BOUNCING BACK!

HOW YOUR SCHOOL CAN SUCCEED IN THE FACE OF ADVERSITY

Jerry Patterson

Janice Patterson

Loucrecia Collins

EYE ON EDUCATION
6 DEPOT WAY WEST, SUITE 106
LARCHMONT, NY 10538
(914) 833-0551
(914) 833-0761 FAX
www.eyeoneducation.com

Library of Congress Cataloging-in-Publication Data

Patterson, Jerry L., 1944–
    Bouncing back! : how your school can succeed in the face of adversity / by Jerry Patterson, Janice Patterson, and Loucrecia Collins.
      p. cm.
    Includes bibliographical references.
    ISBN 1-930556-34-9
    1. School improvement programs—United States.
2. Educational leadership—United States.   3. School management and organization—United States.
I. Patterson, Janice, 1945–   II. Collins, Loucrecia.   III. Title.

LB2822.82 .P38 2002
371.2'00973—dc   2001059783

Also available from Eye On Education

**STRATEGIES TO HELP SOLVE OUR SCHOOL
DROPOUT PROBLEM**
Franklin Schargel and Jay Smink

MOTIVATING AND INSPIRING TEACHERS
The Educator's Guide For Building Staff Morale
Todd Whitaker, Beth Whitaker, and Dale Lumpa

TEACHER RETENTION
What is Your Weakest Link?
India Podsen

HANDBOOK ON TEACHER PORTFOLIOS
For Evaluation and Professional Development
(Includes CD-ROM)
Pamela Tucker, James Strong, and Christopher Gareis

**COACHING AND MENTORING FIRST-YEAR AND
STUDENT TEACHERS**
India Podsen and Vicki Denmark

STAFF DEVELOPMENT
Practices that Promote Leadership in Learning Communities
Sally Zepeda

HUMAN RESOURCES ADMINISTRATION
A School-Based Perspective 2/e
Richard E. Smith

SCHOOL COMMUNITY RELATIONS
Douglas J. Fiore

**CREATING CONNECTIONS FOR BETTER SCHOOLS:
HOW LEADERS ENHANCE SCHOOL CULTURE**
Douglas Fiore

BANISHING ANONYMITY
MIDDLE AND HIGH SCHOOL ADVISEMENT PROGRAMS
John Jenkins and Bonnie Daniel

THE SCHOOL PORTFOLIO TOOLKIT
A Planning, Implementation, and Evaluation Guide
for Continuous School Improvement (Includes CD-ROM)
Victoria L. Bernhardt

About the Authors

Dr. Jerry Patterson is currently on the faculty in Educational Leadership at the University of Alabama at Birmingham. In his more than thirty years of experience as an educator, he has served as a superintendent, assistant superintendent, elementary school principal, and high school teacher. He has authored five nationally recognized books and published more than two dozen articles in professional journals. Dr. Patterson has conducted workshops and presentations throughout the United States and in Slovakia, Isreal, Nepal, Ecuador, Spain, and Canada in the areas of leadership, resilience, and organizational change. Dr. Patterson can be contacted at the School of Education, University of Alabama at Birmingham by phone at 205-975-5946; or e-mail at jpat@uab.edu.

Dr. Janice Patterson has more than thirty years' experience in education at all levels, from preschool to adults, and in urban, suburban, and rural contexts. She has done research on resilience for teachers and schools, educational policy, and school-university partnerships. She has published widely in her field and Dr. Patterson is currently on the faculty in Elementary Education at the University of Alabama at Birmingham. She can be reached at the School of Education, University of Alabama at Birmingham, by phone at 205-934-8365 or by e-mail at JanPat@uab.edu.

Dr. Loucrecia Collins is currently on the faculty in Educational Leadership at the University of Alabama at Birmingham. During her 24 years in education, she has served as a teacher, lead teacher, assistant-principal, and principal in elementary schools. Dr. Collins is known nationally for her with work with conflict resolution programs. In addition, she researches issues of personality type and effective school leadership. Dr. Collins may be reached at the School of Education by phone at 205-975-1984 or by e-mail at lcollins@uab.edu.

Table of Contents

Introduction

This book is written for school leaders: school principals, teacher leaders, school district administrators, and others, such as members of school site councils, who have a stake and an interest in helping schools move ahead in the face of adversity. In other words, the term school leaders isn't confined to just administrators. Throughout the book we provide leadership guidelines that can be used by teaching staffs, school improvement teams, and teacher leaders, as well as by principals.

Bouncing Back! tackles the tough issue of adversity and frames it with a positive question: "How can leaders help their schools move ahead in the face of adversity?" Inherent in this question is our firm belief, based on solid research and documented best practices, that schools can indeed move ahead despite adverse conditions. You may wonder why we have chosen to include adversity as a theme. The following example provides insight into our reasoning.

Recently we began a workshop on resilience for school leaders by asking participants to jot down changes that have affected them professionally over the past three years. After about ten minutes, we called for their responses. Not surprisingly, the school leaders produced pages of chart paper filled with changes, including topics such as more state standards, more children from impoverished conditions, special education legislation, school violence, shortage of teachers and administrators, published school report cards, increase in lawsuits, decrease in parental support, technology explosion, and dwindling resources.

Next we asked, "Given what you have offered as changes in the recent past, as you look ahead to the next three years do you think that the rate and complexity of change will decrease, stay about the same or increase?" We called for a show of hands on each of the three choices, and guess what? Over 90 percent of the school leaders projected that the rate and complexity of change in the future will increase! And over 85 percent of the changes identified were changes being done *to* the schools, not *by* the schools. In other words, the identified changes were imposed changes that created adverse conditions for teaching and learning. Although the results of the quick poll did not surprise anyone, the message seemed to catch some people off-guard.

The message is this: Given the pages of chart paper devoted to changes that have occurred in the past three years, in the next three years there will be even more changes, more adversity, than we've just been through. Therefore, compared to three years from now, today is the "good old days."

We used this activity to make several points. First, a lot has happened *to* schools in the past three years. Second, even more is going to happen, with more intensity, in the next three years. Third, for school leaders to help their schools bounce back from these adverse conditions and become better than their leaders ever imagined, school leaders at all levels will need to demonstrate some very specialized leadership strengths.

The focus of this book, therefore, is on leadership strengths. Its basis is our extensive qualitative research in schools with a demonstrated track record of dealing with adverse conditions. These schools also have a solid history of high performance under tough conditions. We have interviewed school principals, teacher leaders, and classroom teachers to learn firsthand the leadership strategies in place in these high-achieving, high-adversity schools. Throughout the book we draw from real-life struggles by actual school leaders and real schools that looked adversity squarely in the face and prevailed. In order to elicit the highest level of candor from those we interviewed, we guaranteed anonymity. So school leaders and schools are identified by pseudonyms. However, the experiences are real, and so are both the agony and the joy contained within the experiences. From these experiences, as well as our extensive review of the research on resilience, *Bouncing Back!* gives you concrete strategies for implementing the Seven Leadership Strengths of Resilient School Leaders.

In chapter 1, "The Deeper Meaning of Resilience: Achieving Success in the Face of Adversity" we dig beneath the surface meaning of resilience in order to help school leaders:

♦ Contrast the difference between effective schools and resilient schools.
♦ Clarify the target level they want to hit in achieving resilience.
♦ Understand the importance of resilience capacity.

In chapter 2, "Stay Focused on Core Values," we offer help to school leaders in reducing the scatter and increasing the focus on what matters most. We show how you can:

+ Maintain a strong sense of purpose and organizational values.
+ Avoid unnecessary distractions.
+ Maintain perspective for the long haul.

Chapter 3, "Maintain High Expectations for Students and Adults," reminds school leaders that they need to create a school-wide belief that *all* students and *all* adults can succeed, even under tough conditions. We discuss why it is important for school leaders in resilient schools to:

+ Align curriculum and instructional practices with their beliefs about school success.
+ Frequently assess student performance relative to benchmarks.
+ Align supervision and evaluation practices with high expectations.
+ Provide rewards and recognition for success in moving toward the high expectations established.

Chapter 4 emphasizes a critical leadership strength: "Create a Climate of Caring and Support." We describe how school leaders we interviewed helped everyone feel emotionally supported when adversity hits the school. We capture strategies that school leaders use to:

+ Provide a safe environment for teaching and learning to occur.
+ Provide professional support through materials, time, and money even when budgets are tight.
+ Offer personal support to staff and students who struggle through adversity.

In chapter 5, "Take Charge!," we make a distinction between taking charge under so-called normal conditions and under conditions of adversity. We highlight real-life strategies that resilient school leaders use to:

+ Recognize when action is needed and then act quickly.
+ Act on the courage of personal convictions in spite of the risks.

+ Develop and implement approaches to move ahead
  under stressful circumstances.

Chapter 6, "Remain Flexible in How You Get There," builds a
case for the special importance of being flexible in adverse conditions. We offer concrete strategies for how school leaders can:

+ Recover quickly from setbacks when loss happens.
+ Develop skills to be flexible during Tweener Time.
+ Work within imposed constraints to move the school
  ahead.

Chapter 7, "Be Positive in Spite of Adversity," draws on the
most current research and the best practices of school leaders we
interviewed. Resilient leaders shared with us strategies they use
to remain positive:

+ Expect the world to be filled with disruptions and
  don't be surprised.
+ Think "How can we?" rather than "We can't."
+ See the payoff at the end and model a positive attitude.

In chapter 8, "Create Meaningful Participation and Shared
Responsibility," we discuss the difference between token participation and shared responsibility for the future direction of the
school. We provide specific strategies to help school leaders:

+ Resolve the best ways to make group decisions.
+ Reconcile the power struggles over "who decides who
  decides?"
+ Develop ways to train school staff in consensus-building
  strategies.

Chapter 9, "Putting It All Together! The Collective Power of
the Seven Strengths," underscores the importance of how the
Seven Strengths work together to help your school move ahead
in the face of adversity. We also illustrate through concrete examples how the absence of any single strength can weaken the
dynamics of interaction. In this chapter, we remind readers that
putting it all together requires the strong leadership of teacher
leaders as well as the administrative leaders in the organization.
Together, they indeed can help their schools to move ahead in the
face of adversity.

We want to underscore that this book does focus on moving
ahead within the special circumstances of adversity. Some readers may question whether ours is a very optimistic view of lead-

ership. In reply, we offer the words of Václav Havel, the former leader of the Czech Republic. He argues that there is a difference between optimism and hope. Optimism is the belief that things will turn out as you would like. Hope is the belief in yourself that you will fight for what is right and just, irrespective of the outcomes.

We happen to believe that there is ample reason for hope. Our nation does have courageous schools and school leaders who are fighting for what's right and making it, against all odds. We do have leaders in these schools who have not given up hope and who daily promote resilience in the face of adversity. Our commitment in this book is to describe strategies these leaders use so that others in comparable contexts can also gain strength and increased hope. In other words, you, too, can become more resilient than you ever imagined.

1

The Deeper Meaning of Resilience

Achieving Success in the Face of Adversity

Like many other sensationalized topics that grab public attention for brief periods then vanish, the topic of resilience runs the risk of overuse, abuse, and disappearance. For instance, since beginning this book we have seen "Resilience" used as a brand name for panty hose and face cream. The trait of resilience has been attributed to the entire spectrum of human performance, ranging from individuals, such as Lance Armstrong, to entire communities, such as New York City. Disparate interpretations of this thing called resilience help pollute the true meaning of the term. And when the pollution sets in, the concept disappears behind a smokescreen of slogans.

To keep the word *resilience* from falling victim to the prediction "this too shall pass," in this chapter we dig beneath the word to present a research-based framework to help you

- Distinguish between effective schools and resilient schools.
- Articulate the deeper meaning behind the term *resilience*.
- Understand the power of resilience capacity in moving schools ahead.

DISTINGUISH BETWEEN EFFECTIVE SCHOOLS AND RESILIENT SCHOOLS

It is well established that high expectations, high performance, and a supportive context characterize effective schools. Not surprisingly, the research on resilient schools points to a similar set of variables. At first glance, then, it may appear that effective schools and resilient schools are synonymous. But there is a fundamental difference. School resilience certainly embodies school

3

effectiveness, but it also has a deeper and broader meaning. Resilient schools are effective performers that operate within a context of high expectations, strong support, and an empowering environment *even in the face of adverse conditions*. Schools that continue to move ahead, within a context characterized by a *relative* lack of adversity (compared to other schools), become the basis for describing effective schools. When you add to the mix an environment of crisis adversity or ongoing adversity, you have shifted your frame of reference to resilience.

EFFECTIVE SCHOOL EXAMPLE

Briarwood High School, a $75 million facility in its second year of operation, is nestled in the midst of a very affluent community. Most of the school board members in the district serve as company executives. The board is stable and stays out of the business of managing the school district. The district's superintendent, now in his sixth year, previously held the position as Briarwood High School principal. The current high school principal, recruited from a neighboring district by the superintendent, is finishing her fourth year in the job. The district is proud of the track record of Briarwood High School. Within a school culture of high expectations for students and staff, over 90 percent of Briarwood's graduates continue in four-year colleges or universities. Briarwood is proud that they offer more Advanced Placement (AP) courses than any other high school in the state. The Briarwood community is also blessed with a district per-pupil expenditure that ranks in the state's top three. With all of their successes, the high school staff and school leaders continue to look for ways to improve teaching and learning at the high school. Clearly Briarwood High School is moving ahead.

RESILIENT SCHOOL EXAMPLE

George Washington Carver High School is located next to a public housing project, three miles away from Briarwood. At Carver High, 75 percent of the students live below the poverty level; 68 percent have lived in one-parent families within the last three years. With leaky roofs and trailers in the back lot to relieve some of the overcrowding, Carver High has about $5,000 per pupil as the basis for its budget. This is less than half of what Briarwood receives.

Despite these adverse conditions, Carver High School principal Dr. Lamont Jackson is proud of the school's track record. Based on state figures, Carver students are projected to score at about the 45th percentile on state-required tests. The actual scores for Carver High School have been steadily increasing over the past five years to the point where this year the average score was at the 70th percentile. About 40 percent of the students go on to college, up from 8 percent five years ago. As principal, Dr. Jackson puts in long hours to make sure the school stays on track. He is committed to creating a total school environment of caring and support, an environment that includes high expectations for everyone. His commitment has paid off with a stable staff and national recognition as a Blue Ribbon School by the president of the United States.

The principals of Briarwood and George Washington Carver are both effective principals. But the leadership strategies necessary to sustain a high school's continuous improvement in the face of ongoing adversity aren't identical to the strategies necessary to sustain a high school's continuous improvement in much more stable conditions. Imagine what would happen, for instance, if the Briarwood principal were transferred to Carver High School. Leadership strategies that work in an "effective school" setting don't necessarily transfer to a setting of adversity. These comments are not intended to value one set of skills over another. And the comments are not intended to convey that the Briarwood High Schools across the nation are devoid of adversity. Our main point is that there is a difference between effectiveness and resilience. In this book our primary focus is on resilience defined as *using energy productively to achieve goals in the face of adverse conditions.*

ARTICULATE THE DEEPER MEANING BEHIND THE TERM *RESILIENCE*

In the beginning of this chapter, we briefly mentioned the potential danger of polluting the concept of resilience by bundling together all studies that choose to use the word. To sharpen the focus in studying resilience, we strongly believe that school leaders, as well as researchers, need to be explicit and clear about what concepts are contained in the word. We believe this can be achieved by asking two questions.

Question 1: What is the *target level* we want to hit in achieving resilience? Based on our research, school leaders' resilience is interpreted in various ways. Specifically, resilience can be viewed as having three possible target levels. 'People or organizations can be characterized as resilient if they are (1) just getting by; (2) getting back to the status quo after experiencing adversity; or (3) getting ahead through consistent improvement or consistently high performance.

To illustrate the point, imagine that three schools across the nation recently experienced the tragedy of a school shooting. Emerson High School takes the approach "Our goal is to survive this crisis without the school community coming apart at the seams." The school operates in survival mode, continually struggling with its grief. Morale remains low as Emerson High School struggles to hold itself together.

East High School, facing a similar crisis, commits itself to a target of returning to "normal." The goal is for the school to overcome adversity by restoring the school culture to the condition before the crisis.

Poindexter High School embraces a different approach. Learning from the pain of the crisis, they believe they can eventually be even stronger than they were before the event occurred. The Poindexter staff and community set their sights on moving ahead, not surviving or merely getting back to the status quo.

Understanding the target level you hold is central if you are a school leader committed to resilience. In our view, and as documented by substantial research, the only long-term perspective that truly reflects the meaning of resilience is the perspective of *moving ahead*. Throughout the book we present strategies on how to make this happen.

Question 2. What is the condition of our adverse environment? In most of the research on resilience in educational settings, adverse school environments are characterized by one of two possible conditions: (1) ongoing adversity and (2) crisis adversity. To contrast the two environments, we again turn to two different schools.

Dade Middle School, set in the middle of one of the poorest housing projects in this large city, starts each day with adversity oozing from its pores. Poor facilities, poor economic conditions, and poor community support combine to constantly challenge the Dade staff and students on a daily basis.

Everest Middle School recently absorbed the shock of the sudden loss of twenty students and three teachers when a chartered school bus on the way to a football game slid down a steep embankment. The entire Everest community struggles to get out from under the pain of this crisis adversity.

In this book, our research focuses on the target level of moving ahead within the context of both crisis and ongoing adversity. In other words, this book is about leadership strategies that help schools effectively answer the question "How can we use our energy productively to move ahead in the face of crisis or ongoing adversity?"

UNDERSTAND THE POWER OF RESILIENCE CAPACITY IN MOVING SCHOOLS AHEAD

Now that we have erected the scaffolding for understanding the concept of resilience, we need to also elaborate on the power of *resilience capacity*. Imagine for instance that your school, creatively named School A, has a resilience capacity today depicted in fig. 1.1. This capacity represents the "resilience points," or the energy, your school has in its tank to move ahead in the face of adversity. Down the road from you is School B, which has a comparable resilience capacity. In other words, both schools today are poised with equal resilience to face the future.

However, as the future unfolds certain dynamics kick in. Your school makes a conscious effort to implement strategies to help your entire staff become more resilient. You search for strategies that minimize the amount of resilience points you have to spend on any adversity you face. For example, you learn not to be surprised, and waste resilience points, when your expectations are disrupted. You also seize the opportunity to grow your resilience capacity by strengthening your skills to handle disruptions when they do occur.

So you minimize the amount of resilience taken out of your resilience account when adversity does happen, and you maximize the amount of resilience you add to your account by adding more skills to your repertoire.

Figure 1.1 Importance of Resilience Capacity

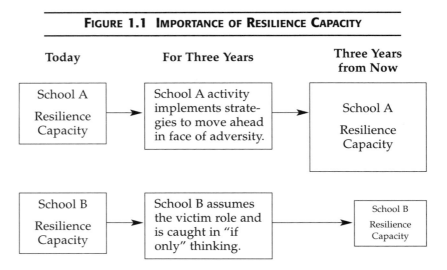

Your buddies down the road in School B take a different approach. They face adversity with all-too-common "if only" thinking. You can almost hear the principal telling the staff, "We could do what is important to us if only those outside the school would quit placing so many new demands on us." By putting themselves in the dependent, victim position of not being responsible for their own organizational health, they place themselves at the mercy of others and continue to deplete their resilience account.

Three years later, your school and School B are ready to face the future. However, each of you is positioned to face future adversity with fundamentally different resilient capacities. As shown in Figure 1.1, your resilience capacity has grown dramatically because of the steps you have taken. Unfortunately, School B, because of the approach it has taken toward adversity, will be tackling the future with a drained resilience account. Imagine the cumulative impact of these dynamics over time. Which school would you prefer to be associated with?

The Seven Strengths of Resilient School Leaders

The concept of resilience that we have presented above draws together what is known from a number of fields, including psychology, education, and organizational management. Our examination of the research literature, plus our own research in ı⌣ school settings, culminated in our identification of the Sev⌣ Strengths of Resilient School Leaders*:

Strength #1: Stay focused on core values.

Strength #2: Maintain high expectations for students and adults.

Strength #3: Create a climate of caring and support.

Strength #4: Take charge.

Strength #5: Remain flexible in how you get there.

Strength #6: Be positive in spite of adversity.

Strength #7: Create meaningful participation and shared responsibility.

In chapters 2–8, we consider each of these strengths separately. We also include the practical strategies, the legs, on which the strengths stand. Finally, in chapter 9 we put it all together to illustrate the dynamic power of the interaction among all seven strengths.

---

* For readers who are interested in the research base supporting the Seven Strengths, we refer you to Appendix A: Research Base for the Seven Strengths of Resilient School Leaders. In addition, you can gain valuable information about resilience in the Recommended Readings section at the end of the book.

2

Stay Focused on Core Values

Recently during a principals' workshop on site-based management, one of the participants was asked if she supported the idea of site-based management. She responded, "It depends."

When pressed about her response, the principal elaborated: "It depends on the year. Each year I ask the teachers to vote on whether or not they want to operate from a site-based model. Depending on the vote, we may or may not be site-based that year."

Whether the topic is site-based management, character education, standards-based curriculum, or whole language, most schools try to be all things to all people, and they end up without focus. In other words they become event-driven, flitting from one innovation to another in search of the magic box that, once installed, will never have to be unplugged again.

When the magic box of, say, site-based management does get installed in the school and doesn't immediately produce the intended results, school leaders predictably pull the plug, scrap that box, grab another, and hope for the best. Eventually the magic boxes accumulate into a junk heap. No wonder that the cynics on your staff see the next box coming and predict—accurately—that "this too shall pass."

This event-driven mentality drains the *individual* resilience of those asked to embrace the newest slogans and drains the *collective* resilience of your school as you struggle to do what is expected of you. Even though staying focused is always hard for school leaders in today's tumultuous conditions, it is particularly difficult to stay focused when you are bombarded by adversity. And it is precisely during adverse times that staff and community need focus the most. To help you focus your energy during adversity, this chapter shows how you can:

- ♦ Create value-driven, not event-driven, organizations.
- ♦ Take the necessary steps to construct core values.

13

• Use core-values packages for periodic assessment.
• Maintain a strong sense of purpose and vision through core values.

CREATE VALUE-DRIVEN, NOT EVENT-DRIVEN, ORGANIZATIONS

Below we present two scenarios to help you discern the difference between event-driven and value-driven schools.

CHALLENGER HIGH SCHOOL, AN EVENT-DRIVEN ORGANIZATION

Challenger High School struggles to make ends meet in this rural area of West Virginia. The economy took a nosedive about a decade ago when the major employer pulled up roots and left town. Community businesses folded and families headed north, where jobs were more plentiful.

Consequently, Challenger High School lost one-third of the student population and budget cuts were severe. But the Challenger High teachers and administrators were a determined group of people. They refused to buckle under adversity. They wanted the best for their students, and they invested considerable energy in finding the best.

For example, the math department read about a program in the *NASSP Journal* called Accelerated Math. The program claimed to supercharge the math curriculum with a new breakthrough in curriculum-management software. The math department made a strong case for implementing this program. With similar zeal, the counselors returned from a workshop called Life Skills Training, a program claiming to cut tobacco, alcohol, and drug use by up to 87 percent. They advocated implementing this program. Next in line were the social studies teachers, who wanted the school to participate in Ted Sizer's Coalition of Essential Schools.

The Challenger High School principal, also determined to make a difference, attended the NASSP Leadership Training Program called Breaking Ranks. He learned how to handle resistance to change, how to strengthen team building, and how to plan and implement strategic initiatives. What he didn't learn was how to make sense of the array of initiatives presented to him. All of the initiatives seemed equally important, so each initiative became just one more "event" to consider in helping the school move ahead.

With the best of intentions, Challenger High School chased a series of events during the five-year tenure of the principal. When the principal left for another assignment, the staff felt they had little to show for all of their efforts except a drained resilience capacity.

WHITTINGTON HIGH SCHOOL, A VALUE-DRIVEN ORGANIZATION

Whittington High School in rural Nebraska offers a strikingly similar demographic profile to Challenger. And, like Challenger, Whittington High is fortunate to have a dedicated staff committed to making a difference under tough conditions.

There is one fundamental difference, though. Whittington staff, including teachers, administrators, and support staff, invested heavily in their own time to chart a course for the future of the high school. They spent evenings, weekend retreats, and summer workshops clarifying the values that matter most to them. Through hard work, frustration, cheers, and tears, they managed to construct core values in areas such as technology, literacy, and student self-esteem.

So when the math teachers came across the Accelerated Math program, they turned to their core values and asked, "Does this program fit with the values that are driving our school into the future?" The social studies teachers and counselors posed the same questions to help guide them in deciding whether to spend their precious resilience points on a particular new program. By clearly articulating a framework of values reflecting what the school stands for, all staff had a template with which to judge how programs contributed (or not) to the values of the school.

The high school principal, in turn, applied what he learned from the Breaking Ranks training to his leadership responsibilities at the school. The processes of team building, handling resistance to change, and implementing new initiatives all were geared to advancing the school's core values. Guiding staff energy in this way actually strengthened school resilience because people had a clear answer to the question "How does this proposed new program contribute to moving ahead according to our core values?"

The two examples above help to distinguish between an event-driven and a value-driven school. Is your school blown by the political winds of the moment, or do you harness the wind by trimming the sails to take you in the direction you as a school have already agreed on?

TAKE THE NECESSARY STEPS TO CONSTRUCT CORE VALUES

If we ended the chapter at this point, you would be justified in saying "So what's new? I'm tired of reading about mission, vision, and values. I've participated in workshops designed to develop our school district's mission statement. In fact, I have a laminated copy hanging somewhere in the school. I just don't remember right now where it is (or what it says)."

But we aren't going to end the chapter at this point. We offer below concrete strategies for moving beyond the mere rhetoric of laminated mission, vision, and values statements.

BE CLEAR ABOUT CORE VALUES

As with its companion words "vision" and "mission," the proliferation of writing about "values" has diluted the word's true meaning to the point where people have different ideas of what it means. To help turn things around, establish a common understanding of core values as they relate to building resilient schools. For our purposes, core values are defined as statements of your convictions, expressing *what you care deeply about*. Core values are not observations, forecasts, or facts. They are philosophical statements that guide your intentions, your actions, and the outcomes of your actions.

At the school level, core values help answer such questions as:

- ◆ Who are we?
- ◆ What do we stand for?
- ◆ What business are we really in?
- ◆ What matters most to us?

In summary, core values become the philosophical basis for clarifying *why* you and your school do what you do. As a school staff, you require students to enter and exit through specific doors.

You require students to walk, not run, in the hallways. You require students to leave dangerous objects at home. You require these things not because you like making rules. You require them because of something deeper your school cares about, perhaps because you value creating a safe environment where all students can learn.

Similarly you create school improvement councils not because you need another set of meetings to attend. You do it because you value forums for open discussion about how the school can be better than anyone ever imagined. When you are clear about what you value, cherish, and care deeply about, you can be more clear to others about what matters most.

UNDERSTAND THE CORE VALUES HIERARCHY

Constructing a core values hierarchy is a way of determining the values that are most central to defining who you are and what you stand for. The core values hierarchy proposed for educators consists of these three levels:

♦ Ethics
♦ Core educational values
♦ Topical educational values

Ethics are core values that specifically express what you believe about what is right and what is wrong. These values may be traced to your deep religious faith or anchored to a nondenominational spirituality that guides you. In either case, ethical values tend to center on universal themes such as compassion, love, integrity, trust, and honesty. These are some examples of core ethical values:

♦ I value acting in a trustworthy way.
♦ I value demonstrating compassion for all people.

When you run into the inevitable conflict between various values you hold, the deep-rooted core values you hold about right and wrong take precedence over your other values.

Just as personal ethics guide your own conduct, *core educational values* guide your overall practice. School districts in general, and schools in particular, exist to improve teaching and learning. Core educational values, therefore, center on what you value about excellence in teaching and learning. School leaders need to be clear and consistent in these values. Sample core educational values include the following:

- We value organizing our teaching strategies around the most current research and best practices.
- We value a school environment that holds all adults accountable for all students achieving at the highest level possible.
- We value creating a teaching and learning environment that emphasizes to everyone that we believe in you, you can do it, and we won't give up on you.

Indeed, the school leaders we interviewed put students first in all matters. They didn't just talk about it—They did it! For instance, Ms. Sorenson, an elementary school principal, said that all teachers know she puts "kid agendas" in front of "adult agendas." As an example, Ms. Sorenson said that a teacher came to her complaining about the choice that his colleague seventh grade teachers had made regarding mathematics texts. Ms. Sorenson reminded him that he was part of the decision-making process and that the selected text was the best match for the students' reading level and for correlation with the curriculum. The teacher responded, "I know but I have been using this other text for ten years now. I don't want to change."

Ms. Sorenson acknowledged his frustration and thanked him for his candor. She also didn't budge from the "kids first" agenda.

Throughout our conversations with resilient leaders, we detected a fine line and, at the same time, a significant difference between being stubborn and being unwavering about what matters most. Especially in adverse conditions, resilient leaders can't send confusing signals about what is most important. A teacher leader summed up the feelings of many of her colleagues across the country: "In order to stay focused on what matters most, you first have to be singularly clear on what it is that matters. In our school, it's academics and safety of students. Everything else is a distant second."

The third level of values in the core values hierarchy centers on *core values about specific educational initiatives*. Unfortunately, with the best of intentions, many schools latch on to the hottest topic of the moment and rush to implement it immediately. Examples of hot topics in the past few years include block scheduling, site-based management, whole language, standards-based curriculum, and portfolio assessment. As the Challenger High School example cited earlier highlights, school leaders and their schools pay a price when they rush to install the solution without first being clear about their core values.

To illustrate the importance of constructing core values for specific educational initiatives, let's examine the topic of site-based management.

Assume your school says it is a site-based-management school. What are the philosophical values that your school endorses, the values that lead you to conclude site-based management is right for you?

Different schools likely will have different responses, but below is a general snapshot of core values directly related to the educational initiative of site-based management:

- We value involving people in school decisions that affect their professional lives.
- We value the input from those holding diverse perspectives.
- We value creating forums so all voices can be heard in a safe environment that is free of retaliation or retribution.

By constructing core values about this specific educational initiative, your school moves from an event-driven approach regarding site-based management to a value-driven approach. In other words, your school *invests* its collective energy in a common set of values rather than *wasting* individual energy chasing individual interpretations about the meaning behind the slogan *site-based management*.

CONSTRUCT CORE VALUE PACKAGES

Even if your school does start by constructing core values rather than chasing labels, you may end up with a problem. You will assume the process is completed with the completion of the value statement. However, there is still a missing link.

For instance, suppose your school develops the following core values to guide instructional practice:

- We value placing a central focus on improving learning for all students.
- We value creating a school climate of high expectations for all students to perform up to district standards.

+ We value implementing teaching strategies consistent
  with the latest research and best practices about effective teaching.

Each of these values meets the test of a core value. Each con-
veys something your school believes strongly about teaching and
learning.

However, as mentioned earlier, there is a major missing link.
Imagine that you were part of the school team who crafted these
important core educational values. You complete your work on
Tuesday afternoon at a staff meeting. What do you do on
Wednesday morning to begin implementation of these values?
More importantly, what do you as a total school staff agree should
be done in the classroom based on what you declared as impor-
tant in the value-development process?

ADD THE POWER OF *WE WILL* STATEMENTS

Construct a set of *we will* statements that describes specifically
what you as a school will do in practice to make your core value
come alive. The *we will* statements give added meaning and depth
to your philosophically oriented value statements. The *we will*
statements also present a public declaration of what people can
expect from you because of what you value. Finally, these statements provide a solid basis for holding people accountable for acting consistently with what is valued.

Decatur Middle School decided to use the framework presented
above to construct a core value package for a core value related to
improving student learning. Below is the product of their efforts.

CORE EDUCATIONAL VALUE:
IMPROVING STUDENT LEARNING

+ We value placing a central focus on improving student
  learning for *all* students.

Therefore we will:

+ Constantly convey that staying the same is not good
  enough.
+ Implement strategies for charting and clearly communicating the progress of each student to staff, the
  student, and parents of each student.

- Incorporate diverse teaching strategies that are responsive to the diverse learning styles among our children.
- Mobilize virtually all of our school's human resources around the theme of improving learning.
- Set budget priorities based on our commitment to improving student learning.
- Avoid instructional fads and other distractions that take us away from our central focus.

In the above example, Decatur Middle School has a unified focus on the *how* of implementing the core value. For any specific educational initiative you tackle, you can accomplish the same effect by combining the strength of core value statements with the specific direction created by *we will* statements.

To make sure you are on the right track in developing core value packages, ask yourself the following questions:

- Does the value statement clearly and specifically articulate what we stand for and what is important to us?
- Do the *we will* statements reflect what our school will actually do as a process to help move us from just the idea level to the stage of implementing the idea?
- Does the core value package clearly convey to those outside our school what they can expect from those of us inside the school?

If your school takes the actions outlined above, you have taken huge strides to focus on what matters most. However, there is still work to be done.

USE CORE VALUE PACKAGES TO COLLECT PERIODIC FEEDBACK

In our work with organizations across the globe, we rarely find instances where the organization has taken all of the steps we outlined above. Most organizations stop short of moving the value statements to the more specific level of articulating the "*we will*" statements. Even more rare are the organizations that use this core-value package to periodically gather formal and informal feedback about how well they are doing to align their practices with their values. Below we outline a three-step feedback cycle.

Step 1: Collect data on importance and implementation effectiveness. Let's suppose that two years ago your school did, indeed, develop the comprehensive core-value package outlined above on improving student learning. Two years later, how do you know how well you are doing relative to what you value? And, perhaps more important, how do you know the values are still important now? One way to answer the question is to convert the core-value package into a brief feedback inventory. As shown in fig. 2.1, Importance Inventory, and fig. 2.2, Implementation Effectiveness Inventory, you can ask two important questions for each value and *we will* statement:

- ♦ To what extent is this statement still important to us (fig. 2.1)?
- ♦ To what extent are we effectively implementing the statement in our daily practice (fig. 2.2)?

**FIGURE 2.1 TOPIC: CORE VALUES ABOUT STUDENT LEARNING
IMPORTANCE INVENTORY**

Instructions

On a 1–5 scale, indicate how important each key point below is to you.

1	2	3	4	5
not important		somewhat important		highly important

Importance	Key Point
	Place a central focus on improving student learning for *all* students.
	Constantly convey that staying the same is not good enough.
	Implement strategies for charting and clearly communicating each student's progress to staff, the student, and parents of the student.
	Incorporate diverse teaching strategies that are responsive to the diverse learning styles among our children.
	Mobilize virtually all of our school's human resources around the theme of improving learning.
	Set budget priorities based on our commitment to improving student learning.
	Avoid instructional fads and other distractions that take us away from our central focus.

FIGURE 2.2 TOPIC:
CORE VALUES ABOUT STUDENT LEARNING IMPLEMENTATION
EFFECTIVENESS INVENTORY

Instructions
On a 1–5 scale, indicate to what extent you have effectively implemented each key point below.

1	2	3	4	5
not implemented		somewhat implemented		highly implemented

Effectiveness	Key Point
	Place a central focus on improving student learning for *all* students.
	Constantly convey that staying the same is not good enough.
	Implement strategies for charting and clearly communicating each student's progress to staff, the student, and parents of each student.
	Incorporate diverse teaching strategies that are responsive to the diverse learning styles among our children.
	Mobilize virtually all of our school's human resources around the theme of improving learning.
	Set budget priorities based on our commitment to improving student learning.
	Avoid instructional fads and other distractions that take us away from our central focus.

Drawing on the data you collect in the Importance Inventory, your school can answer the question: "Has the importance of any of these statements changed during the time since we constructed them?" If so, start the cycle all over again, because you don't want to spend your resilience points implementing words on paper that you no longer value. Realistically, if the values truly are core values, it is unlikely that you will find yourself abandoning them on a regular basis.

More likely, based on the data you glean from the Implementation Effectiveness Inventory, you will find that that you need to pay attention to implementation of some of the statements in the core-value package. Specifically, look at the discrepancy scores between the strength of the value (how important is this to us?) and the practices (to what extent are we effectively implementing this?). We amplify what this looks like in the next step.

FIGURE 2.3 GAP ANALYSIS INVENTORY

Key Point	Importance	Effectiveness	Gap
Place a central focus on improving student learning for *all* students.	5	4	1
Constantly convey that staying the same is not good enough.	4	3	1
Implement strategies for charting and clearly communicating to staff, students, and parents the progress of each student.	5	3	2
Incorporate diverse teaching strategies that are responsive to the diverse learning styles among our children.	5	2	3
Mobilize virtually all of our school's human resources around the theme of improving learning.	4	3	1
Set budget priorities based on our commitment to improving student learning.	5	3	2
Avoid instructional fads and other distractions that take us away from our central focus.	4	4	0

Step 2: Conduct a gap analysis to identify areas for follow-up action. When you analyze the data, look for the areas with the greatest discrepancy between importance and implementation effectiveness. Suppose, for instance, your school completes all of the steps outlined above. After tabulating all of the data, you distribute your results, shown in fig. 2.3, to the staff. At this point, look for the greatest gaps between importance and effectiveness. According to the data, the greatest gap exists on the following point:

• Incorporate diverse teaching strategies that are responsive to the diverse learning styles among our children.

So this point becomes your focus for developing an action plan
for improvement.

Step 3: Use gap analysis as a basis for action. By constructing a task/timeline framework like the one outlined in fig. 2.4,
you and your school staff can build action plans to make the core
value become reality.

Figure 2.4 Action Plan

Topic	Improving Teaching and Learning
Goal	Incorporate diverse teaching strategies that are responsive to the diverse learning styles among our children.

Task	Timeline	Leadership Responsibility	Resources Needed	Indicators of Accomplishment

The steps we have outlined provide specific strategies for:

• Collecting data on the importance and implementation effectiveness of core values you hold.
• Conducting a gap analysis to identify areas for
improvement.
• Developing action plans to close the gap between
importance and implementation effectiveness.

At the end of each of chapters 3–8, we will revisit this three-
step process by encouraging you to collect periodic formal feedback on one of the Seven Strengths of Resilient School Leaders.

THE ADDED POWER OF PERSONAL REFLECTION

As a complement to the rather structured approach to gathering feedback on the alignment of values and practices, school
leaders can gain a deeper understanding of their values and

practices by carving out the necessary time to engage in personal reflection. Along with the formal feedback sections at the end of chapters 3–8, we conclude each chapter with a series of questions for informal reflection to be used by school leaders. The combined power of formal feedback and informal, personal reflection gives you a solid foundation for moving ahead on each of the Seven Strengths.

MAINTAIN A STRONG SENSE OF PURPOSE AND VISION THROUGH CORE VALUES

LEADERSHIP RESPONSIBILITIES

In addition to constructing core value packages and collecting feedback, school leaders have other very important leadership responsibilities to help the school stay focused on core values. A recurring theme throughout this book is that leadership strategies that seem so basic and straightforward strain under the weight of adversity. Your consummate challenge is to confront the question "How can I do what is necessary and expected regarding core values when our school is up to our neck in alligators?" Below we present three concrete strategies to help answer the question.

RESIST THE TEMPTATION TO CHASE NEW INITIATIVES

Many school leaders told us they try not to swing with the pendulum of new fads. As one principal reported, "Everything new that comes across my desk either gets tossed or filed for another day. I am not putting anything else new on my teachers. Not at all! I have a staff that is focused and I feel my role is to support them in what they are doing, rather than adding something else to their plate."

Another principal said she waits to see if the newfangled idea has legs. "When someone comes to a principals' meeting with a suggestion about a new idea, I don't take it back to the school right away. I make certain it has legs. Too many times we spend unnecessary resilience points worrying, when there is nothing we can do."

The principal was quick to tell us, however, that once the idea actually grows legs, she moves from protector to informer. In her words:

> "When it becomes clear that we are going to have to do something, I almost fall into the category of too much information. People need to know how things work, what's going on. And I don't let them whine about how we're going to get this cancelled because it's not going to get cancelled. If the teachers have concerns about how this new thing with legs will impede their success, I want to know about it. But I am not going to be an obstructionist, once the district has made a decision."

BUFFER OTHERS FROM UNNECESSARY DISTRACTIONS

Resilient leaders uniformly protect their staffs from anything that even hints at pulling the teachers away from putting their highest priority on student learning. A high school principal described his role as buffer in rather poetic terms: "I try to protect them from the storm. When the storm hits, I try to be the tree that bears the brunt of the storm, so the teachers receive less damage."

Other school leaders offered concrete strategies about how they serve as a buffer against distractions.

- ◆ "I want them teaching, not doing paperwork, so I am dogged about them not doing paperwork."
- ◆ "We only allow one announcement during the day and that's in the morning. Otherwise, it had better be an emergency."
- ◆ "I work as a sieve, so things just don't get to the teachers."
- ◆ "I don't disturb teachers in the classroom when instruction is going on."
- ◆ "I keep the central office mumbo jumbo out of the school."
- ◆ "Our social services staff, the nurse, plus the counselor help to meet the nonacademic needs of the students, so that the academic teachers stay focused on what we're all about."

MODEL ON A DAILY BASIS WHAT YOU STAND FOR

All of us have experienced school leaders who can talk a good game about purpose and vision. They can even hold high expectations for others. But the true test of making the grade is when school leaders take the step of consistently modeling the vision and purpose they so strongly advocate. And, of course, the modeling becomes even more difficult when the going gets tough. Without exception the resilient school leaders we met were indeed role models. One principal modeled her values by spending about two hours on the interview process for new teachers:

> "I invest this much time because I am going to have to live with that person, and this is a student's life that is at stake here. There isn't anything in this school that is more important than the selection of the teacher for those students. Teachers make the difference. And therefore we won't settle for anything less than the best."

Modeling also takes the form of consistently letting people see your passion for what you do. And, as the school leaders report, your passion had better be genuine, because staff and community can see through phony passion in a heartbeat. We were touched by the deep commitment to children we found in many of the schools we visited. Representative of the passion expressed by resilient leaders were the words of this highly motivated teacher leader: "My resilience is strengthened because I love what I am doing. Children are my passion, without question! I have a strong belief that we can make a strong difference in the life of a child."

Summarizing the sentiment of the fire in the belly of the school leaders, one leader put it succinctly: "My job is to do whatever it takes, I mean literally whatever, to help the students and teachers be successful."

Our job in this chapter has been to describe strategies that help stoke the fire in your belly to do what it takes to stay focused on what you care about.

COLLECT FORMAL AND INFORMAL FEEDBACK ABOUT LEADERSHIP

The process we have described throughout this chapter gives you "hard data" to assess the steps necessary to stay focused on core values. A second dimension we mentioned earlier is informal, personal reflection by you. Specifically, we recommend that you reflect on the following questions.

INFORMAL REFLECTION BY SCHOOL LEADERS

- How extensively have I focused on being a value-driven, not event-driven leader?
- How have I applied the values hierarchy in deciding what matters most?
- To what extent have I constructed core value packages, including values and *we will* statements, for basic educational values and specific educational topics?
- How have I used core value packages as a basis for collecting periodic feedback about importance and implementation of core values?
- In what ways have I used data to develop and implement action plans for aligning values and practices?
- How have I helped the staff resist temptations to chase new initiatives?
- How have I buffered others and protected myself from unnecessary distractions?
- In what ways have I regularly modeled for others what I stand for?

3

Maintain High Expectations for Students and Adults

Throughout our research on resilient schools, two words separated the highly resilient schools from those that are not resilient: No excuses! This theme bounced off the walls and echoed through the conversations we had with each of the school leaders in resilient schools. In the words of one school leader, reflecting the sentiment of many of her colleagues across the United States, "There are absolutely no excuses for failing to produce achieving students. None. Zero. Zilch. I mean *no excuses.*"

Clearly such powerful words leave no room for misinterpretation and no doubt about the expectations driving the school. In fact, "No Excuses" has become the campaign slogan of at least one national organization founded to mobilize public pressure on behalf of better education for the poor. A major challenge for school leaders operating under adversity is to move the "No Excuses" from mere slogan to concrete reality. The purpose of this chapter is to examine in depth how school leaders facing adversity can effectively implement high expectations for students and staff. Specifically we will describe leadership strategies about how to:

- Create a schoolwide belief that all students and staff can succeed.
- Maintain high expectations for students and staff even during tough times.
- Align instructional and supervisory practices with beliefs about school success.
- Frequently assess student and staff performance relative to benchmarks and follow-up with appropriate actions.
- Provide rewards and recognition for success in moving toward the high expectations.

In the first half of the chapter we will focus on students, then we will shift our focus to staff in the second half.

CREATE A SCHOOLWIDE BELIEF THAT ALL STUDENTS CAN SUCCEED

If you are a leader in a school facing chronic adversity, then the odds are good that many students who enter your doors aren't profiled as high achievers. These children face such overwhelming conditions outside of school that there's not always energy left to focus on learning. Even in the face of these obstacles, however, we discovered resilient schools who relentlessly acted on the value that *all* students can succeed.

To help your school act on this value, apply the steps in chapter 2 for constructing core values. Here is a sample core value package related specifically to student success for all students:

Value:

We value placing a central focus on student success for *all* students.

Therefore We Will:

- ♦ Constantly convey that staying the same is not good enough.
- ♦ Implement strategies for charting and clearly communicating progress of each student to staff, student, and parents of student.
- ♦ Incorporate diverse teaching strategies that are responsive to the diverse learning styles among our children.
- ♦ Mobilize virtually all of our school's human resources around the theme of success for all students.
- ♦ Set budget priorities based on our commitment to student success.
- ♦ Avoid instructional fads and other distractions that take us away from our central focus.

DETERMINE STAFF READINESS TO IMPLEMENT THE CORE VALUES

As you begin to move ahead on the core value outlined above, you can anticipate that the levels of staff readiness will fall into four categories:

1. Staff who genuinely embrace the value and are making it happen.
2. Staff who genuinely embrace the value but their practices don't always reflect it.
3. Staff who support the value with a conditional yes.
4. Staff who are non-believers.

Let's look at each category and potential actions for you to take.

STAFF WHO GENUINELY EMBRACE THE VALUE AND ARE MAKING IT HAPPEN

Continue to offer them support and encouragement, as well as opportunities to model their practices for others. These individuals are valuable assets in helping others achieve success for all students. One veteran teacher leader described modeling in her school:

> "Not all teachers are created equal. We pair weak teachers with more successful teachers so the weak can become stronger. They can learn how to manage a classroom, work with parents, and create daily lessons from the defined curriculum. The end result of this ongoing staff development is improved teaching."

So, for staff who genuinely embrace the value and are making it happen, find out what support they need, turn them loose, and get out of their way.

STAFF WHO GENUINELY EMBRACE THE VALUE BUT THEIR PRACTICES DON'T ALWAYS REFLECT IT

Apply the process outlined in chapter 2 for collecting feedback. When you identify gaps between values and practices, staff who fall into the category described above will likely recognize the gaps and willingly, although somewhat painfully, make the necessary adjustments to achieve alignment. Just remember that sometimes it is a slow and difficult journey for staff who have good intentions and struggle to come to terms with the reality that some of their practices don't match their stated value. So be patient and continue to provide the feedback and related data that help these well-intentioned staff see the discrepancies for themselves.

STAFF WHO SUPPORT THE VALUE WITH A CONDITIONAL YES

If some staff members say they believe all students can succeed except under certain conditions, then the answer isn't yes, which means the value is rejected. This isn't a matter of semantics. It is a serious question that needs to be resolved before the school can move ahead on the theme of high expectations. Resilient leaders (both formal and informal leaders) acknowledge that students may come with a lot of disadvantages and that it is the leader's job to help them learn no matter what it takes. An urban middle school principal said it this way: "We need to get rid of the baggage and excuses and focus on the notion that these students come to us to learn. We are responsible for them. No yeah-buts!"

For the staff who are the "conditional" believers, be steadfast in your expectations of success for *all* students with no conditions attached. In addition, solicit suggestions from the conditional believers regarding the support, information, and resources they need from you and the rest of the system to help them implement the school's expectations for success. Obviously, within reason, you need to supply the help they say they need. Finally, hold the conditional believers accountable for becoming believers in *all* students succeeding and for adjusting their teaching accordingly.

STAFF MEMBERS WHO ARE NON-BELIEVERS

This category may range from veteran teachers waiting for retirement to new teachers who come unprepared for the challenges they face. How do you move ahead when some staff members blatantly announce that they don't believe all students can succeed?

If the non-believers are few in number, work with them in a supportive way so they can feel adequately prepared and justified in endorsing the school value.

Several principals told us that they always place a successful, veteran teacher on each grade level. Then if the team gets discouraged and starts saying they can't teach "these" kids, it's the successful teacher's job to say, "Oh yes you can, and let's figure out how." This strategy lets the non-believing teachers know that you expect them to be successful and that you are there to help. It also reinforces for the doubters the idea that success for all is not just the leader's expectation; it's also the expectation of their colleagues. Peer pressure can work well in setting expectations that all students can succeed and that all teachers can teach for success.

If your conversion attempts fail, you need to be publicly and persistently resolute in your own belief that it is not acceptable, after repeated attempts to help, to have these people continue working in your school. Several school leaders we interviewed addressed this point directly and unequivocally:

> "I tell them, "'You may not philosophically agree with what I'm asking, but we are going to move ahead. You are either with us or against us. You decide."' You can't create a false belief that any philosophy about expectations is okay."

An even more daunting challenge is what to do if the non-believers are in the majority in your school. If you plan on staying at the school under these conditions, be resolute in your expectations. As one principal reported:

> "As long as I am principal in this school, you can be assured that I will not waver in my belief and expectation that all people, students and adults, can succeed in this school. More pointedly, I expect you to believe and act on the premise, *I believe in you, you can do it, and I won't give up on you*. I expect this to pervade everything you do in this school. The bottom line is, No Excuses! Everyone can succeed."

The choice to take the hard-line approach regarding expectations does not come easily, and it does not come without a price. If the dominant school culture currently operates counter to your belief, then a lot of resilience points will be spent trying to make a shift in the school culture. Anticipate this and decide if the price is worth paying, both for you and for those undergoing the pain of change.

Another choice is to conclude that the school culture does not match your belief system. Under these circumstances, you may need to exit the culture and find one that is a better fit. This choice is painful, too. School leaders in general are not known as quitters and you are no exception. One way to resolve this issue is to make sure you have invested considerable energy trying to turn around the culture before you decide that the price isn't worth the effort. In the final analysis, however, if you come to the decision to leave, do it without guilt or a feeling of failure. There are times when each of us needs to recognize when the fit is in reality a misfit and it's time to move on. In the long run, this can be a resilience-building move for you.

MAINTAIN HIGH EXPECTATIONS FOR STUDENTS EVEN DURING TOUGH TIMES

Once again, it is relatively easy to "walk the talk" during normal conditions. But what happens when tough times hit? In this case, when tough times happen (and they will), those school leaders who are firmly committed to the belief of high expectations for students will remain tough in their demand that high expectations will not be compromised.

Suppose, for example, you are the principal of a high school that has enjoyed three years of consistently rising test scores. The high school also enjoys the benefit of a community that consists primarily of college-educated and well-paid parents. It has been relatively easy for the high school staff to live up to the self-generated schoolwide belief of high expectations for all students.

This year things are different. A new high school just opened in the district, and redrawn school attendance boundaries have resulted in a shift in demographics. Some of the affluent neighborhoods in your school area have been shifted to the new school and you have been assigned two low-income neighborhoods. Over half the new students failed the district's benchmark exams in English and mathematics.

Given this reality, now what do you and the staff believe about high expectations for all students? In other words, schoolwide beliefs are going to be tested by the fire of adversity. Our true beliefs emerge when we stand tall and committed to these beliefs even during tough times. A natural tendency is to slip into the victim role when adversity hits. We say we want to hold to a certain belief, but right now we can't because we are a victim of circumstances. But true beliefs aren't situational. As a school leader, be resolute that victim status is not an excuse at any time, especially when it comes to standing firm on expectations for students even during tough times. A staff that is committed to high expectations works very hard not to let students see themselves as victims when the going gets tough. Teachers and administrators relentlessly emphasize strategies that help students figure out *how can I make it through this adversity* rather than slip into the mindset *I can't make it through this adversity.*

ALIGN INSTRUCTIONAL AND SUPERVISORY PRACTICES WITH BELIEFS ABOUT SCHOOL SUCCESS

The alignment of curriculum with instructional practices is both very logical and very difficult. Of course it makes sense to align curriculum and instructional practices with core values about expectations for student success. Of course your school wants to do the right thing. The difficulty lies with what lies beyond the statement of commitment. In other words, if your school commits to the path of aligning practices with values, you are going down the path of examining how you currently practice your craft. And this examination means you will likely have to confront gaps between values and practices. In turn, this means you are faced with the realization that some things you have been doing need to be changed and some new things need to be added to your practices.

From a logical perspective, all of this makes sense. From a human emotion perspective, not many of us relish examining our conduct in light of our values because of the possible pain in what we discover. As a school leader, anticipate this difficulty as your school examines alignment of practices and values. Applying the action steps we outlined in chapter 2, when the inevitable gaps pop up, continue to assure staff that their values are in the right place and that the gaps just indicate areas in which you can be better than you ever imagined.

It's also important to emphasize the value-added approach instead of the repair approach. Gaps do not mean that the people or systems are broken. Gaps simply illustrate what we already know. No person, no school is perfect. So celebrate the successes that you have and also take the steps necessary to move ahead on the continuous improvement continuum.

FREQUENTLY ASSESS STUDENT PERFORMANCE RELATIVE TO BENCHMARKS AND FOLLOW UP WITH APPROPRIATE ACTIONS

Without a doubt, benchmarks and student assessment are hotly debated topics. Almost every state is embroiled in the politics of these issues. Our purpose is not to argue over the who, what, and why of establishing standards and holding schools accountable. Our purpose is to establish the links between high expectations, classroom practices, and assessment and the need to modify practices as appropriate to support student achievement. The ultimate goal is for student achievement to be congruent with high expectations.

THE IMPORTANCE OF FREQUENT ASSESSMENT

In our research conversations with resilient school leaders, they were adamant in their unwavering support for frequent assessment of student performance. A teacher leader in a middle school represented many leaders when she said bluntly, "I don't oppose the state testing. It causes the teachers to have to be accountable to teach the curriculum." Over and over again, school leaders told us that schools can't afford to be uninformed about student progress. They also told us that student progress needs to be measured frequently and measured directly against the established benchmarks. One leader we interviewed for this book was unapologetic about the emphasis her school places on testing:

> "We do massive assessments in this school, both formal and informal. These assessments are keyed to very specific skills. Any day, any hour of the day, I should be able to go in and pull up the data on where every child is on a

specific skill. Focus means not waiting until you get the results data to take action. My advice to other principals? You need to know, instructionally, what is going on in the building all of the time."

These school leaders don't waste their resilience points complaining about standards being imposed from above. They just get about the business of monitoring student progress. An elementary principal told us that assessment begins very early in the year in her school so that teachers know where to begin teaching the students. She explained:

"We know where the kids are in October. As painful as it is to be assessing in the fall the students' possibility of making the assessment targets in the spring, it is less painful than getting to the end of the year and the students not meeting the benchmarks."

In schools like these, the leaders take deliberate steps to make student assessment part of the culture of the school. In some cases, particularly where there may be teacher resistance to state-mandated testing, leaders use humor to acknowledge the negative feelings and move beyond them. One example came from a teacher leader in a large elementary school who told us about one of her school's strategies: "We had a party for teachers called 'Slam-Dunk the [state mandated test].' We had an after-school gathering with milk and cookies. We were told to write down everything we hated about the testing, wad up the piece of paper, and slam-dunk it." She went on to say that these actions seemed to help teachers get beyond their resistance and move ahead to focus on getting students ready for the exam.

FOLLOW UP ON ASSESSMENT BY ADAPTING TEACHING PRACTICES

Leaders were quick to point out that the real value of testing comes when the school staff follows the assessment with solid record keeping and immediately begins to create and adjust instructional strategies as necessary. As we discuss in chapter 6, "Remain Flexible in How You Get There," school leaders and school staff need to be ready to modify their practices in order to get where they want to be. In resilient schools, responding to low scores is frequently a collaborative effort, often involving teacher leaders directly in the classroom:

"When our third grade testing scores weren't where they should be, we said we need to have some flexible strategies to get where we need to be. So our peer facilitators [teacher leaders] came in and taught on a regular basis. The third grade team used this time to come up with its own plan."

At the secondary level, a middle school principal described his school's practices regarding student assessment beyond the required statewide tests:

"Student performance is regularly monitored and refined through weekly tests in all subjects every Friday. The students maintain written journals, which promote an interdisciplinary approach to their studies and provide a portfolio of their progress across subject areas."

Teachers in the school supported this emphasis on assessment and adapting instruction. As one teacher put it, "This is the three-part sequence of my formula for success: immediate personal attention, testing, and adapting my instruction to the results of the test. End of story."

CREATE A SCHOOLWIDE BELIEF THAT ALL STAFF CAN SUCCEED

With the same passion and spirit that you convey to students the belief that all students can succeed, convey this message to staff about their own success. Especially during adversity when some staff members start doubting their own ability to make a difference, show by your actions that "you are important, I care about you and I will help you." This common message needs to be received equally across the spectrum of employment categories.

The school leaders we interviewed were adamant about creating a positive climate based on a strong belief that all staff are capable of succeeding, even in the face of difficult times. And the successful schools' definition of *staff* included all who work in the building. Resilience cuts across job titles in creating an environment where people do their jobs well, in part to support the efforts of others. Whether it's the school librarian, the secretary, or the lunchroom supervisor, all staff need to know you respect what they do, that you know that they face a tough challenge under adverse conditions, and that there are high expectations for their performance.

MAINTAIN HIGH EXPECTATIONS FOR STAFF EVEN DURING TOUGH TIMES

A No Excuses school means no excuses for adults as well as students. School leaders will be the first to acknowledge that they walk a tightrope trying to balance the belief in adult success at their school with the accompanying belief in no excuses for failure. However, you can't have a successful school without both dimensions. A belief in adult success without high expectations for achieving that success results in blurred vision about what is acceptable performance by teachers and other staff. In contrast, a school environment that demands high expectations for performance without an accompanying climate of believing that the staff can succeed results in poor morale and likely in poor performance by staff and students. So the tightrope is there waiting for you. As a school leader, do whatever it takes to negotiate the tightrope successfully.

A middle school principal solved this dilemma by personally working with all his teachers. Every morning at 7:30 he meets for a weekly conference with a teaching team from different grade level. The time is set aside to address instructional issues and individual (student and teacher) performance. He makes his expectations and his willingness to support teachers very clear:

> "I support my teachers to use whatever materials they find that works. The only time it gets questioned is when it stops working. It's sort of like coming from a wealthy home, though. If all you have ever eaten off of is china, instead of plastic ware, that is the norm. Do the teachers appreciate my support? Yes. Do they know I expect them to perform? You bet."

This principal went on to tell us that he sees his job as supplying teachers with whatever they need to improve their instruction, even if that means finding funds for outside seminars or additional supplies. Equally clear was his message that expectations do not waver, and the teachers know it.

ALIGN SUPERVISORY AND EVALUATION PRACTICES WITH BELIEFS ABOUT SCHOOL SUCCESS

As the saying goes, what gets measured becomes what's considered important. Once the core values are in place, the benchmarks have been established, and curriculum and instruction practices aligned, it logically flows that the expectations for staff are set, too. To effectively complete the picture, supervision and evaluation practices need to coincide with the expectations for teachers that, in turn, coincide with the expectations for students.

Putting this cycle in place is difficult under the best of conditions. Under adverse conditions, the difficulty level rises dramatically. However, the leaders of resilient schools argue that under adversity it becomes even more important to hold firm on evaluating staff performance in a manner consistent with the high expectations established. Otherwise, there is a natural tendency to start looking around for reasons to explain why students aren't performing. With the framework outlined in this chapter, looking around isn't acceptable. The looking begins within one's self as instructor of the students.

FREQUENTLY ASSESS STAFF PERFORMANCE RELATIVE TO BENCHMARKS AND FOLLOW UP WITH APPROPRIATE SUPPORT AND TRAINING

If frequent assessment is important for students, then it is important for staff as well. Note, though, that assessment doesn't translate into judgment. Assessment of performance means providing feedback on performance so necessary adjustments can be made quickly. Students who come to school every day with the proverbial deck stacked against them can't afford to waste any opportunity for quality teaching and learning. If a teacher is struggling in certain areas of his or her teaching, the teacher needs to know about it so that two things happen promptly. First and foremost, school leaders need to get the instruction back on track as soon as possible because everyone involved has a lot at stake in the success of these students. Second, the teacher needs to receive the necessary support and training to help with the problem areas.

One principal described her strategies for frequent assessment of staff, and quick intervention to benefit the students and the teacher. She makes it clear from the very beginning that students are expected to meet benchmarks established by scores from the previous year. She tells teachers that she expects, at a minimum, the same level of achievement or beyond. She tells them that she will do all she can to support them and that she expects them to keep her informed of their needs and any issues that could derail student achievement. The teacher evaluation system is aligned with state standards. The teachers are told that they will be evaluated each year on two of the categories within the state standards. The principal selects one of the categories and the teacher selects the second one. She also describes her grading system:

> "I made it clear that on a 1–4 scale, 4 is exemplary and hard to get. The criteria for getting a 4 is, first, that you would be willing to share the skill by doing a seminar for staff on that category; second I need to have seen it, and I need to remember it! A 3 indicates strong proficiency; 2 signals a need for help. I work hard to give 4's in the categories they want me to observe. In areas where the teacher scores a 2 or below, I work extra hard to provide support and training to bring the teacher up to our high expectations."

The principal went on to comment that, after repeated attempts to be supportive prove unsuccessful, it's time to "bite the bullet." She discussed with us a situation where she had to remove a teacher who, despite repeated made over several months by the principal, teacher leader and grade level chair, made no progress: One of our teachers is now leaving. I told the teacher two months ago that, if you want to stay here, your performance on the next assessment has to look differently than it does now. She expended no effort and did not improve."

For this principal, the cost to students was too great not to take action and remove the teacher. She moved her out of the classroom and gave her another job in the school for the rest of the year. Classes were reconfigured to cover the loss of that teacher.

Throughout our visits to research sites, school leaders were united in their views of the serious drain on resilience caused by teachers who can't or won't meet expectations. They were unanimous in their conviction that keeping morale up during times of adversity is tough and that the best medicine is student success. As long as students are progressing in step with expectations, there's little problem with morale. A middle school principal told us:

> "The only time I see a problem with morale is when a teacher comes here and is not carrying his or her own weight. Other teachers know that they are giving 110 percent and they can't carry any more. They will come to me and say, '"He either needs to get with the program or get out'."

"Get with the program or get out" is indicative of the non-negotiable stance this principal and others take on the role of aligning teacher assessment with student learning.

Speaking of non-negotiable stances, one school we visited took huge strides toward holding high expectations for students and adults when the school created a Commitment to Excellence Pledge. As shown in fig. 3.1 this pledge holds parents, students, and staff publicly accountable for their role in contributing to student learning. Acknowledging that this is a bold and risky step, the school leaders reported that such a measure clarified the high expectations and the no excuses climate that permeated the school.

FIGURE 3.1 COMMITMENT TO EXCELLENCE PLEDGE

Teacher's Pledge
- I pledge to arrive at XYS School every day by 7:15 A.M. (Monday–Friday).
- I pledge to remain at XYZ School until 4:30 every day.
- I pledge to attend activities at XYZ School on appropriate Saturdays and evenings. I will arrive when activities begin and remain until they are finished.
- I pledge to teach at XYZ School during the summer term.
- I pledge to teach in the best way I know how and I will do whatever it takes for our students to learn.
- I pledge to always make myself available to students and parents, and to respectfully consider any concerns they have.
- I pledge to always protect the safety, interests, and rights of all individuals in the classroom.
- I understand that failure to adhere to this pledge can lead to my dismissal from XYZ School.

Teacher   Principal

Parents'/Guardians' Pledge

- I pledge to make sure our child arrives at XYZ every day by 7:25 A.M. (Monday–Friday) or boards the school bus at the scheduled time.
- I will make arrangements so that our child can remain at XYZ School until 4 P.M., Monday–Friday.
- I will make arrangements for our child to come to XYZ School on appropriate Saturdays and evenings. Our child will arrive when activities begin and remain until they are finished.
- I will ensure that our child attends summer school.
- I will always help our child in the best way I know how, and I will do whatever it takes for him/her to learn. This also means that I will check our child's homework every night, let him/her call the teacher if there is a problem with the homework, and try to read with him/her every night.
- I will always make myself available to our children and the school, and to address any concerns they have. This also means that if our child is going to miss school, I will notify the teacher as soon as possible and I will read carefully all the papers that the school sends home.
- I will allow our child to go on field trips
- I will make sure our child follows the XYZ dress code.
- I understand that our child must follow the XYZ School rules so as to protect the safety, interests, and rights of all individuals in the classroom. I, not the school, am responsible for the behavior and actions of our child.
- I understand that failure to follow these rules can cause my child to lose various XYZ School privileges or spend time in detention, and can even lead to my child returning to his/her home school.

_____   _____
Signature   Signature

Student's Pledge

- I pledge to arrive at XYZ School every day by 7:25 A.M. (Monday–Friday) or board a XYZ bus at the correct time.
- I pledge to remain at XYZ School until 4:30 P.M. every day.
- I pledge to attend activities at XYZ School on appropriate Saturdays and evenings. I will arrive when activities begin and remain until they are finished.
- I pledge to attend XYZ School during the summer term.
- I pledge to always work, think, and behave in the best way I know how and I will do whatever it takes for me and my fellow students to learn. This also means that I will complete all my homework every

night, I will call my teachers if I have a problem with the homework or a problem with coming to school, and I will raise my hand and ask questions in class if I do not understand something.

- I pledge to always make myself available to parents and teachers and to respectfully consider any concerns they have. If I make a mistake, this means I will tell the truth to my teachers and accept responsibility for my actions.

- I pledge to always behave so as to protect the safety, interests, and rights of all individuals in the classroom. This also means that I will always listen to all my XYZ School students and give everyone my respect.

- I will follow the XYZ School dress code.

- I am responsible for my own behavior and I will follow the teachers' directions.

- I understand that failure to adhere to this pledge can cause me to lose various XYZ privileges or spend time in detention, and can lead to my returning to my home school.

Student

And it should be noted that this school points with pride to an exemplary track record of success in working with students from extremely adverse circumstances.

PROVIDE REWARDS AND RECOGNITION FOR SUCCESS IN MOVING TOWARD THE HIGH EXPECTATIONS

In schools filled with adversity, school leaders can't wait until the annual state reports come out to celebrate successes. Because the work is so exhaustively demanding for students and staff, celebrate the small wins along the way. At the classroom level, look for any reason possible to celebrate student achievement at any moment. One example came from a fourth grade teacher who told us how she talks with individual children about their scores as a way of encouraging them:

"Even if a child doesn't make a passing score, we celebrate the gains made. I know I can move a child 12 to 15 points a year, and a normal gain is 9. So I say to the child, look at the progress you have made; if you keep doing that at the end this is where you are going to be. Because the child has to have some hope too. Small wins. Also it gives me a target to shoot for. Because I know that I can pull the child up."

At the school level, find ways to honor progress in your journey to improved student learning. When the whole school shows progress, then have a whole-school celebration. When departments, grade levels, or individual teachers achieve breakthroughs in their instructional approach or when their students hit the mark, find ways recognize and reward their efforts. Some of the strategies used by school leaders to recognize teacher success were not what we anticipated. For instance, one principal sends the spouses of successful first-year teachers a thank-you note saying, "Thanks for letting your spouse give so much of his/her time to the school this year. Hopefully you will get more time next year than I." The aim is to let teachers and spouses know that the principal recognizes how much time that teachers put in.

Another principal told us about her notes to parents *of the teachers:* "I have sent notes to my faculty's parents, and they really love it. When you, as a forty-year-old, find out that your parents have received a note on what a great job you did, it's very gratifying." Other tactics included recognizing teachers in faculty meetings, writing them notes, and putting small gifts in their boxes, including some that were meant to symbolize what the teacher's work meant to the children. For instance, one teacher leader distributes geraniums to teachers on the last day of school with a note comparing the growth of a flower to the growth of students in their classes during the academic year.

Teachers confirmed that individual attention from a school leader for a job well done means a great deal: "I really don't need a gift or a happy gram. What I like best is when she [the principal] stops by my room to see what I'm doing and talk to me about it."

The main focus of this chapter has been on high expectations and strong accountability measures for those who teach and learn in high-stakes environments. We realize, to the extent that we can without actually working in your high-stakes school, that difficulties abound in trying to reach the expectations laid out here. We also realize that too much is at stake to lower the bar. Schools throughout the United States and beyond have cleared the bar of high expectations and high performance for everyone. As a school leader, you can do it, too.

COLLECT FORMAL AND INFORMAL FEEDBACK ABOUT LEADERSHIP TO MAINTAIN HIGH EXPECTATIONS FOR SUCCESS

In chapter 2, we developed in detail a process you can readily use to collect feedback about successful implementation of the leadership strengths necessary for moving schools ahead in the face of adversity. In fig. 3.2, we present Feedback Inventory on High Expectations, a form you can apply to the specific leadership strength of maintaining high expectations for success. You can use the key points contained in the Feedback Inventory or you can modify the points to fit your circumstances and core values.

In addition, school site councils and school staffs can use the same inventory format to get feedback on what the school stands for regarding high expectations and how the school is going to move ahead on this priority.

As a second dimension to your feedback process, you can ask yourself the following questions:

INFORMAL REFLECTION BY SCHOOL LEADERS

- In what ways have I created a schoolwide belief that all children can succeed in adverse conditions?
- How have I articulated and maintained high expectations for students during tough times?
- How have I provided leadership to align curriculum and instructional practices with beliefs regarding school success?
- To what extent have I led our school to assess student performance relative to benchmarks and adapt appropriate instruction and curriculum?
- In what ways have I created a schoolwide belief that all staff can succeed in adverse conditions?
- What have I done to articulate and maintain high expectations for staff during tough times?
- How have I aligned supervision and evaluation practices with the expectations?
- To what extent have I assessed staff performance relative to benchmarks and followed up assessments with appropriate support and training?

FIGURE 3.2 FEEDBACK INVENTORY ON HIGH EXPECTATIONS

Instructions: For each key point, record your rating on a 1–5 scale.
To indicate the level of *importance* you attribute to each key point, record the rating in the *Importance* column.

1	2	3	4	5
not important		somewhat important		highly important

To indicate the extent to which the key point has been *effectively implemented*, record the rating in the *Effectiveness* column.

1	2	3	4	5
not implemented		somewhat implemented		highly implemented

Compare the ratings to determine the *gap* between importance and effectiveness.

Key Point	Importance	Effectiveness	Gap
Create a schoolwide belief that all children can succeed in adverse conditions.			
Articulate and maintain high expectations for students during tough times.			
Align curriculum and instructional practices with beliefs regarding school success.			
Assess student performance relative to benchmarks and adapt appropriate instruction and curriculum.			
Create a schoolwide belief that all staff can succeed in adverse conditions.			
Articulate and maintain high expectations for staff during tough times.			
Align supervision and evaluation practices with the expectations.			
Assess staff performance relative to benchmarks and follow up assessments with appropriate support and training.			

4

Create a Climate of Caring and Support

In our research on resilient schools, we found some schools where the adults were supported, nurtured, even spoiled a little bit. On the other hand, students in the schools were not extended the same support. They trudged to school each day to an emotionally non-supportive environment. In contrast, other schools we visited held students in the highest regard, and treated the adults as second-class citizens. The truly resilient schools we attended maintained a healthy balance of showing caring and support for both adults and students. In this chapter, we discuss strategies that resilient school leaders use to:

- Provide caring and personal support for adults.
- Show caring and personal support for students.
- Create a safe environment for teaching and learning to occur.
- Provide instructional guidance.
- Provide direct access to needed materials.
- Provide the gift of time.
- Find the money to fund the priorities.
- Collect formal and informal feedback about leadership to create a climate of caring and support.

PROVIDE CARING AND PERSONAL SUPPORT FOR ADULTS

As we work with school districts throughout the United States and beyond, we typically ask school groups, "What are the things you need most from the system?" Virtually without exception, among the top three needs that school groups express is this: "We need to feel like the system cares about us as human beings, not just placeholders and faceless names on the organization chart. We need to feel a sense of caring regarding our hopes, fears, and tears."

Although the actual response to the question about needs isn't surprising, we have been somewhat surprised by how universally the need for caring is expressed. The need to be cared for and supported is near the top of the list for all groups, irrespective of class, gender, and geography. So the plea is clear: People need to feel cared for and emotionally supported.

The response to the plea is just as clear: Provide care and support. With such simple messages and simple answers, why do individuals and groups still feel like these needs aren't being adequately met?

PROVIDING CARING AND SUPPORT IN
NORMAL VERSUS ADVERSE CONDITIONS

Let's return once again to the distinction between providing caring and support in schools during "normal" conditions and meeting these needs under "adverse conditions." The examples below illustrate our point.

Suppose you are a school leader in a suburban school district that is recognized throughout the state as a top performer. Your school has been blessed by a stable, highly educated community with low mobility, strong parental support, and a tax base reflected in one of the highest per-pupil expenditure rates in the state. Teachers in your school, which opened just a year ago, applied to become part of the new school culture. You enjoyed the luxury of being able to handpick those applicants who fit the vision of where you want to take the school.

Teachers have ample supplies, excellent support staff, shiny new classrooms, and, therefore, very little reason to leave. Although stress, personal crises, and interpersonal conflicts are not foreign to the school, you, as a school leader, have comparatively favorable conditions for providing caring and personal support.

We use the term *comparatively* because one mile down the road you cross your school district boundary lines and enter another world—a world of urban challenges. Once upon a time, this world looked different. The city was known for its diverse population, strong economic base, and strong, proud schools. Slowly at first, then more rapidly later, the minivans filled with Anglo families crossed the magic divide into your school district, leaving one world to create another.

In its wake, the mass exodus to the suburbs left the city with declining economics, schools segregated by race, and decaying support for education. So one mile from your shiny school, there is another dedicated school leader with dedicated teachers. In contrast to your conditions, though, these adults have to deal with large class sizes, leaking roofs, a highly mobile community, and some of the lowest teacher salaries in the state. Support staff are a rare commodity. And these school leaders have the same responsibility and dedication as you do to create a climate of caring and emotional support. They have to do it, though, in *comparatively* more adverse conditions.

The above example is not intended to discredit or cause guilt for your school's comparatively favorable conditions. The example is presented to highlight the special challenges faced by school leaders under adverse conditions in their attempts to build and sustain a climate of caring and support. However, even if you don't fit into the category of *comparatively adverse conditions*, the strategies we discuss below have direct application to your environment as you strive to provide caring and support for everyone.

USE THE POWER OF PERSONAL CONNECTIONS

Caring for your staff begins with a personal connection. As mentioned at the beginning of the chapter, adults in schools tell us they want to be known as human beings with their own particular joys and fears. So get to know them as people; invite a teacher to lunch and have someone take her class. Talk to her about what's going on with her children and her elderly aunt who lives with her.

Take the time to learn the names and interests of family members. Recall how you feel when your supervisor takes the time to ask about your son or daughter who just left for college. Similar feelings stir when you stop by the history classroom and ask, "How was Maria's birthday party on Saturday?" Or, if you know that one of the teachers grows exotic orchids, a magazine article on Hawaiian orchids delivered to him demonstrates that you know and care about him as a person.

When you reach out to a teacher during a time of personal crisis, the gesture is long remembered and can convey a rich message of caring to the person and the larger school community. A teacher leader in an urban elementary school described what happened when she learned that a terminally ill teacher was resigning at the end of the year:

> "I organized a garage sale of all her teaching materials and teacher-made materials she had accumulated from twenty-eight years of teaching. Others helped. We priced things and let everyone know about it. A lot of people came and bought her materials. She got all the money and lots of hugs and thank-yous from people who cared about her."

As well as sending impromptu notes to adults, one principal we interviewed took deliberate actions, planned in advance, to show all school staff caring and support.

> "My assistant principal and I make a plan at the beginning of the year. We know that once a month we are going to target something. It's on the calendar to do. It may be an Easter gift, or a poem, but nine times a year this is going to happen. Also we show we care about individual teachers as well. If a teacher gets nominated for teacher of the year, it goes up on the bulletin board, and announced at the faculty meeting."

MAKE CARING AND SUPPORT A PART OF THE SCHOOL CULTURE

Recently we saw a cartoon depicting two tired sailors adrift at sea, seated at each end of a seven-foot life raft. Unfortunately the life raft had sprung a leak about two feet from one of the sailors. The other sailor said with a smirk on his face, "I'm sure glad the leak isn't on my side of the raft."

From your perspective as a school leader, you can see very clearly that "we are all in this boat together." Despite the isolation of teachers in classrooms, all adults and students in the school are in the thick of adversity together. No wonder that teachers and school leaders tell us so adamantly that building strong camaraderie among staff is crucial to helping the school move ahead. To maintain resilience in a school facing adversity, the combined strength of the individual members adds up to a total that is greater than the sum of the parts. In other words, it is not just a cliché to say there is strength in numbers. There also is strength in diversity. Some staff members are known and appreciated for their ability to bring the perspective of wisdom accumulated through age. Young staff members come with new, off-the-wall ideas that may be the fresh breeze needed when things are getting stale. Others bring the strength of perspective built from living in a particular culture. Still others bring the strength of scars earned from living through incredible adversity. Camaraderie comes from seizing on these diverse strengths in a collective commitment to helping the school move ahead.

In an urban district facing difficult space issues, one high school teacher we interviewed talked about how the district demonstrated its concern for all staff:

> "They shut down the schools for a day and everyone who worked for the school district was invited. We were all bused to one location and you got to see everyone in the whole school district. There was a motivational speaker and food for us. I think that went a long way in showing that they do care about us and that we are important."

In a time of dwindling resources or in low-income districts, an extravaganza like the one above may not be financially possible, so you may have to be creative in developing a solution to demonstrate organizational caring. As we emphasize repeatedly, however, it is even more important during times of reduced funding and other external rewards to work hard to demonstrate that you care about people. Even if you resort to a potluck dinner and entertainment by the high school band, it symbolizes caring and support.

SHOW CARING AND PERSONAL SUPPORT FOR STUDENTS

In a community overflowing with adverse conditions, students bring the effects of adversity to school with them. Adults in these schools use strategies such as those described below to show their caring and support.

CREATE A WELCOMING ENVIRONMENT

As we moved among the schools to conduct our interviews, it became clear that in a resilient school where people care about children, there are immediate, visible clues. The environment is inviting. For example, buildings are made as attractive as possible. In one crumbling urban school, a beautiful student-painted mural of the rain forest was so inviting that we didn't notice the crumbling plaster. Sure, the plaster needs repair, but the reality is that it may not happen for a while. So the principal and staff found creative ways to make the walls say "We care about you."

GIVE PERSONAL ATTENTION

Adults in these schools use a variety of strategies to let students know they are valued and supported and, in the process, to build students' resilience. As one member of our research team walked through a middle school with a large, muscular male principal, she noticed that he called many children by name and asked them specific questions about their lives. At one point he stopped and called out to a young man named Demetrius. When Demetrius came closer, the principal asked for his mother's phone number. The student's eyes widened with concern and he asked what he'd done to get in trouble.

The principal pulled out his cell phone and standing right there with the student at his side, he called the mother and said, "Mrs. Wynn, this is Mr. Miner at Forest Park Middle School. I wanted to call and tell you that I just reviewed all the exhibits in the science fair and Demetrius did a wonderful job with his volcano. He worked very hard and I'm proud of what he did and wanted you to know."

In one sixty-second phone call, this principal made both Demetrius and his mother feel important and let them know that he cared about them. Even in the midst of all the adversity in their lives, we doubt they'll ever forget that call and Mr. Miner's care.

MAKE CARING FOR STUDENTS A PART OF THE SCHOOL CULTURE

Resilience-building school leaders plan for a schoolwide culture of care and support for students. Students are actively taught to ask for help when they need it, and they get it. One of the most glaring examples of caring for students we found was in a high school where teachers committed themselves to be on call to students twenty-four hours a day. All the teachers wear beepers and give out their home telephone numbers. Students are expected to call if they are confused about an assignment. As one student describes the plan: "After I do the homework, I can actually call the teachers to get the answers. The teacher might give me a mini quiz over the phone to be sure I understand what's going on. I know a lot of students who have calling plans for math."

No excuses are accepted for failing to complete homework, and, at the same time, the students have no doubt that teachers and school leaders care about them.

Understandably, some students face problems too tough for you to fix. Although you can keep your ear to the ground and know when a child needs a coat, you are unlikely to be able to stop violence in the neighborhood. As one teacher leader said:

> "There are times when my greatest act of caring is listening to the child and reminding her of her own resilience and ability to cope. Even in the worst situation, a child can be taught to take pride in her strength. Yesterday, I said to a student, '"I know it's tough for you at home right now, but I think you're real smart to go your neighbor's when your mom and dad start fighting. That's real smart and you're a good problem solver."'"

Realizing that no recipe works to assure that all students will overcome all adversity, we do believe strongly that one little sentence goes a long way to show caring and support for students: "You are important, you can do it, and we will not give up on you."

CREATE A SAFE ENVIRONMENT FOR TEACHING AND LEARNING TO OCCUR

Although you can't do much to control the world outside of school, most resilient leaders work hard to control the inside world. Today, school safety is on all school leaders' minds. With the widespread media attention to school violence and threats to school safety, no one argues about the importance of safe school environments. For some children, school is the only safe place they know.

In the following paragraph, an urban middle school principal describes his own leadership struggle to get a grip on a school out of control.

> "The first three to four years, I concentrated on getting the overage students out of the building and cutting down on the discipline issues. I smile a lot and have an easygoing personality. But when it comes to taking care of business, I have a Jekyll and Hyde personality. You have to take care of business, you have to be hard and tough to let the kids know you care. Caring means giving them a safe place to learn. I want the environment conducive for learning. When I walk down the hallway, I don't want to see kids in the hallway, I don't want to see kids in the classroom disrupting the classroom. Right now, when you go into classes, you will see learning taking place."

As this scenario so richly illustrates, to create a safe learning environment, sometimes you have to start with tough love.

Another example of creating a safe environment can be found in an initiative called "Don't Laugh at Me" (Operation Respect, 2001), based on the core values of expressing feelings in constructive ways; caring; compassion and cooperation; resolving conflict creatively, and celebrating diversity. Peter Yarrow of the folksinging group Peter, Paul, and Mary teamed with Educators for Social Responsibility, the creators of the Resolving Conflict Creatively Program (RCCP), to create this initiative.

Staff at one school involved with Don't Laugh at Me reported that the program content contributed to a safe, supportive atmosphere within the school. Although it focuses on students in elementary and middle schools, staff noted increased communication and cooperation among teachers, too.

PROVIDE INSTRUCTIONAL GUIDANCE

In addition to creating an environment of caring and emotional support for students, school leaders have a responsibility to provide professional support to staff. In this section, we describe how school leaders can demonstrate this support through instructional guidance.

There is a substantial research base on the relationship between self-efficacy and student achievement. In other words, teachers who feel they can make a difference in students' lives usually do. By contrast, teachers who feel overwhelmed by their inability to make a difference instructionally usually live up to their feelings.

Even though low self-efficacy can be found in all schools, the condition can become almost epidemic in school settings marked by ongoing adversity. As students bring their vast and deep needs through the schoolhouse doors, educators face enormous instructional challenges that get magnified in schools operating under tough conditions. With such challenges, the teacher's need for instructional guidance is much more apparent than in conditions of less diversity and adversity.

School leaders can significantly help struggling teachers strengthen their instructional strategies and thereby strengthen student achievement by advocating for the following forms of support:

1. Informal guidance from principal to teacher.
2. Formal sessions with small groups of teachers and the principal.
3. Informal guidance from one teacher to another.
4. Formal guidance from mentors.
5. Formal and informal guidance from teacher leaders.

INFORMAL GUIDANCE FROM PRINCIPAL TO TEACHER

As an instructional leader in your school, it's probably second nature for you to look out for beginners and help those who struggle behind classroom doors. One beginning teacher we interviewed talked openly about his principal's involvement in helping him become a better teacher:

> "The principal is really good about encouraging us. If you are doing something that isn't helpful to the kids the principal will come in and talk to you and tell you it's not working, but in a very sensitive way. She'll suggest that

perhaps you should try approaching the lesson from this angle or that angle."

With no prior knowledge of what this novice teacher had told us, the principal gave this response to our question about what she personally does to provide instructional guidance for struggling teachers:

> "I look back on things that I have used when I first started. For example, the Harry Wong videotapes for teachers who are having discipline problems really helped me when I first started teaching. I also continue to attend instructional workshops, and do a lot of professional reading. I read a lot of Lou Ann Johnson books, and they give a lot of good ideas on how to work with people and how to work with students. If I'm not knowledgeable on current thinking in the content areas, I can't help teachers."

Her message is clear. As a leader intent on providing professional support, she sees her responsibility as staying knowledgeable about content and teaching strategies. We weren't surprised to learn that this principal regularly goes into classrooms and substitutes for her teachers so that they may attend a professional development workshop or visit another school. She promotes resilience and gains credibility with her staff by demonstrating her knowledge and abilities in the classroom.

FORMAL SESSIONS WITH SMALL GROUPS OF TEACHERS AND THE PRINCIPAL

Another principal we met uses a more structured approach. After school he confers with subject-area teams on a rotating basis. He asks what problems they're encountering and offers on-the-spot guidance and suggestions. Sometimes it's to direct a new teacher to a veteran in the building; other times, he suggests a particular text or an instructional strategy.

INFORMAL GUIDANCE FROM ONE TEACHER TO ANOTHER

Instructional guidance frequently comes from another teacher. Most often, it's a casual comment or bit of advice offered in the

CREATE A CLIMATE OF CARING AND SUPPORT   65

teacher's lounge or on the playground. For instance, one beginning teacher told us that the teacher across the hall had cautioned against spending so many hours creating attractive bulletin boards. The veteran advised that much time was needed to prepare lessons for the children and that she didn't want the beginner to burn out. She also gently reminded the beginning teacher that bulletin boards were places where children hoped to see their own work displayed, not the teacher's masterpiece.

Instructional guidance offered kindly and professionally to a rookie by a veteran gives the new teacher the feeling that instructional support is close at hand.

Even veteran teachers receive and give teacher-to-teacher guidance in managing children and classroom instruction. Teachers told us repeatedly that other colleagues were those they most often asked for instructional help, both formal and informal. Grade-level meetings to discuss math curricula, after-school sharing of materials for a literacy project, and the multitude of other ways that teachers lend support to one another not only enhances individual professional growth, but also is an important aspect of staff resilience. Lines of caring and support must connect among the staff if we are to succeed in creating a resilient environment. School leaders who provide a mechanism for busy professionals to connect around kids and content will go a long way toward creating that culture.

FORMAL GUIDANCE FROM MENTORS

According to our interviews, the use of formally designated mentors for new teachers and peer-to-peer facilitation for veteran teachers is happening with increasing frequency in resilient schools. In all the situations we've encountered that use mentors or peer facilitation, the process did *not* include formal evaluation that had any bearing on tenure. Instead, it was designed to provide instructional support and to promote the idea that teaching and lifelong professional development go hand in hand. By including veteran teachers in a peer facilitation process, the message is that all staff will continue to develop professionally.

Although a mentoring program for a new teacher typically pairs the newcomer with a teacher on the same grade level, that's not always the case. A mentor told us about her first-year teacher mentee:

"She's really struggled with the curriculum and also with the personality conflicts on the grade level. I invited her to come by on her off time and show me what she was planning to do. She really felt like she wasn't getting enough help from her grade level. So she would come by during her planning time and ask me what would be a good activity to do to teach a particular skill. Or she'd ask, '"Would you do this with partners or a larger group or individually?"' So, I'd give her ideas and pull materials and helped her that way. I would listen to her vent some of the things that were going on. She's a hard-working teacher; it's just hard to be new and you need to have your hand held sometimes by someone other than your grade-level peers and be told that you are doing a good job."

A middle school principal told us that, because her school has such adverse conditions compared to all other schools in the district, a mentor teacher is assigned to each experienced teacher who isn't new to the profession but just new to the school. "Just because you have some experience teaching, when you come to our school, it can be a whole other world from what you've known before. So, the mentors really help."

Mentors counsel mentees on a variety of issues related to their professional success, such as problem students, course content, paperwork, parking, and the preferences of the principal. Knowing that there's at least one other person in the building invested in your success goes a long way in building staff resilience.

Because of a prior track record of burnout, one district actually allocates funds through the superintendent's budget to invest in mentoring of new teachers. Beginning teachers apply as a potential mentee and agree to work for half salary for the first year. In exchange, they get a portable computer and tuition for a master's degree program, and they are released one day a month to work with an expert in integrating technology in their classrooms. A respected veteran teacher is assigned to a small group of mentees and released from teaching duties for two years before rotating back to the classroom. One mentee teacher said:

"I was incredibly lucky to be accepted as part of the mentor program. I've learned so much. We have meetings with the mentor group every month. I've gotten to know really good teachers in the district and other new teachers. The mentees have really bonded and we've made personal friendships. The mentors help us in any way we need and give us lots of support for our teaching. They give us positive energy. In times of adversity, we know they are always there to help."

FORMAL AND INFORMAL GUIDANCE FROM TEACHER LEADERS

Perhaps as a result of teachers saying repeatedly and in a variety of ways that they learn best from other teachers, several resilient schools have designated formal teacher leaders. Responsibilities vary across schools but the underlying goal in every case we encountered was support for teaching and student achievement. When we asked one principal how the role of teacher leader was defined, he replied that it's determined by the staff:

> "We have a cadre of five people and we can call on these people any way we like to help our programs. I lay out the parameters, and I also am not bashful about saying, "'Staff, here's a political announcement: this is what I think or these are my views.'" Then I turn them loose. They figure out what they would like for the teacher leaders to do."

It's not surprising that the teachers in that school report that the teacher leaders are a crucial resource for the school's success. The teacher leaders also feel good about their contributions to the school:

> "This year, the other peer facilitator and I each taught $1^1/2$ hours a day in one of the third grade classrooms because the third grade team wasn't real strong in math and they needed to see some model lessons. We were proud to be able to make a contribution."

In a subsequent conversation, the principal discussed the difference that the teacher leaders had made in helping to retain one of those same third grade teachers:

> "I have teacher leaders who are strong in math and they went into her class all year and taught math. She watched them develop the concepts and now she can do it. I want

to salvage her because she is very good in other ways, has a real teacher's heart. Teacher leaders are extremely instrumental in supporting the academic focus."

We would add that the energy teacher leaders bring to their colleagues who struggle makes an important difference in staff resilience. A key ingredient of resilience is believing that you can overcome obstacles. Non-threatening, willing, supportive instructional guidance by teacher leaders goes a long way in bolstering the self-efficacy of colleagues. A teacher leader in one southern elementary school said it well: "I'm willing to do anything that they need to help make it easier for them. It just makes everyone's job easier."

In our research, in every school that implemented the teacher leader concept, these dedicated individuals were highly respected for the creativity and resourcefulness they add to the school environment.

PROVIDE DIRECT ACCESS TO NEEDED MATERIALS

In schools facing ongoing adversity, it is commonplace to find a lack of materials available to teachers. In the resilient schools we researched, access to materials happens because it is directly linked to what matters most: student achievement. Schools facing adversity make sure they have their priorities in order. Even if it means sacrificing in other areas, school leaders make sure the school is responsive to the teachers' needs when it comes to instructional materials. This responsiveness is both a substantive and symbolic message: substantive because concrete support to instruction is a top priority; symbolic because it offers concrete evidence of school leaders aligning their practices with their values. If quality instruction is the bottom line, then school leaders will do whatever it takes to make sure the materials are there to support the staff.

Teachers agreed that administrative support in the form of materials makes a difference:

"They're [principal and assistant principal] very good about buying programs and materials we need to help increase our test scores. They set the tone for the rest of the school. That has a lot to do with everyone's attitude, being upbeat and receptive to all these challenges and going with it. They make you want to do it because they are willing to do whatever it takes to help you get what you need to do your job. The message flows from the top down."

Some teachers acknowledged that their access to materials and supplies wasn't typical protocol in other district schools. As one teacher put it:

"If there is something I need, I can go get the funds from the principal to purchase books or whatever materials are needed. There aren't these barriers in our way. Most schools set up these barriers for the teachers; there is a long procedure of red tape to show you need the ten bucks to make a purchase. Maybe in three months you can get it, but for us, it is immediate."

Another teacher in a different school district offered a similar story:

"Supplies? We have unlimited supplies here, even with such poor financial conditions. I hear people talking who teach at other schools and the supplies are all locked up. The supply warden guards them. That just doesn't happen here. We have an open supply closet and we go in and get what we want. We have what we need to do our jobs. It makes us feel like professionals."

Another powerful example of providing professional support involves a different kind of "material:" the keys to the school. One of the principals drew on her own experience to underscore the symbolism of keys:

"We treat our teachers professionally. They have keys to the building. They can come in weekends, nights, anytime. When I was a teacher in another district, I couldn't even get into the building. I vowed that if I ever became a principal that I'd change that and I did."

The message was not lost on the teaching staff. Several teachers in the schools we visited pointed directly to the message of having keys to the building as a major symbol of trust. Working under adverse financial conditions, many times it is easy for teachers and school leaders to slip into the victim status, lamenting the lack of money and materials. Keys to the building is a relatively inexpensive way to build resilience by saying symbolically, "You are important and we trust you."

PROVIDE THE GIFT OF TIME

High on the list of needs by a school staff is the plea for more time. Resilient school leaders place a premium on time. They expect teachers, as well as themselves, to freely give of their time to students and to use that time productively to improve student learning. Teachers tell us they want time to plan, time to make personal phone calls, time to eat with other teachers, time to sit quietly and reflect. And time is often the resource that school leaders find most difficult to give. Yet most of the resilient leaders we interviewed articulated how important it is, practically, politically, and symbolically, to create time for instruction.

One of the most obvious strategies to give staff additional time is the practice of a school leader going into the classroom and teaching the students in order to free the teacher for needed reflective time.

> "When I do this," commented one principal, "the teachers know that I am sacrificing other principal-type stuff that has to be done somehow. So when the teacher sees me lugging home tons of paperwork at night, the teacher knows that I gave to her the gift of time, because I'm paying for the gift by taking my own time late at night to do work that I could have otherwise done at the office."

We recently interviewed another principal who occasionally offers the gift of time by using schoolwide staff development days:

> "Our district staff development days are controlled at the school level. If we have staff development in the full day format, I try to give the teachers a half day in their rooms to see how they want to implement the ideas."

Other principals used community members to monitor lunchrooms, read to children, and in other ways to free teachers. Teacher leaders were also willing to juggle their schedules to provide extra time. We overheard one teacher leader volunteer to take a fifth grade class because the regular teacher's son was hospitalized following a car accident. The teacher had not asked for the time, but the teacher leader knew it would be appreciated. And it was, particularly when it had not been requested but was offered out of a leader's sense of caring and support.

Teachers also told us that school leaders are able to find time for them to develop their lesson plans, attend workshops, and observe outside teaching methods by creative scheduling even during low-budget times. Sometimes teachers will combine classrooms so that one can leave for a professional development seminar. In some instances, particularly with beginning teachers, additional time can be found by helping the newcomer enhance his or her time management skills and focus on what's important. In almost all instances, resilient leaders found ways to make time a valuable resource rather than a scarce commodity.

FIND THE MONEY TO FUND THE PRIORITIES

If there's anything more scarce than extra time in schools that face ongoing challenges, it's money. With state legislatures continuing to reduce funding for schools and a reduction of funds for education at the federal level, the scenario is unlikely to improve. For many, the only alternative is to create options at the local level. Many of the school leaders we interviewed are finding ways to secure "extra" funds and, in the process, to develop resilience among staff.

However, securing funds should not be undertaken without a clear link to purpose. We talked in earlier chapters about the need for aligning actions with core values. Nowhere is this more important than in the area of how money is spent. People watch to see how scarce dollars are spent and who decides how to spend them. Resilient school leaders focus funding on what matters most for students. Often, teachers and other staff are involved in making those decisions and in doing whatever it takes to get the money.

When we asked one teacher leader how her middle school had managed to garner so many more resources than the closest middle school two miles away, she replied:

> "Our extra resources come from grants that we've written. They are out there if you are willing to go after them. Grant writing is a pain to do, but it's worth it . . . I wrote one for the Nature Center and I'd never written a grant before. Our nurse, our former principal, and a retired counselor wrote the one for the clinic. The principal and some people at the administration building put some information together for the grant we received for $175,000. Our school publishes a paper that lets you know what grants

are out there, and if you write a proposal and they [the funding agency] think it's good enough, then you will get the money."

Following this powerful example of entrepreneurship, the teacher leader told us that the person who writes the grant has a large say in how the school uses the money, but other voices in the school are also considered. For instance, when a local oil refinery gave the school $2,000, the administrators asked the teacher-writer and other staff what they thought about how to spend it. Together they decided what was most important for student learning. Rarely is it a one-person decision. By making the expenditure a consensus decision most of the time, the staff buys in to how the money is spent and feels that their opinions matter to the administration.

Across virtually all schools we visited, there appeared to be a sense among the teachers that if there was something they really felt was important for students, resilient leaders will help them find the money. Some even told us that working with other teachers or staff to write a grant had been an important professional growth experience for them and had created some new friendships. They came together around a common goal and helped accomplish it.

We began this chapter with an argument for creating a climate of personal and professional support. We've provided you examples of what we learned from talking with resilient leaders in schools from different parts of the country who carry the attitude verbalized by one school leader: "Despite extraordinarily limited resources, no activity goes wanting at this school if it's good for kids." Applying the principles we've presented, you too can strengthen the climate of personal caring and support in your own organization.

COLLECT FORMAL AND INFORMAL FEEDBACK ABOUT LEADERSHIP TO CREATE A CLIMATE OF CARING AND SUPPORT

Consistent with our earlier recommendations to collect periodic feedback, in fig. 4.1 we offer a feedback inventory form you can use to collect data about the alignment of values and leader-

FIGURE 4.1 FEEDBACK INVENTORY ON CARING AND SUPPORT

Instructions: For each key point, record your rating on a 1–5 scale. To indicate the level of *importance* you attribute to each key point, record the rating in the *Importance* column.

1	2	3	4	5
not important		somewhat important		highly important

To indicate the extent to which the key point has been *effectively implemented,* record the rating in the *Effectiveness* column.

1	2	3	4	5
not implemented		somewhat implemented		highly implemented

Compare the ratings to determine the *gap* between importance and effectiveness.

Key Point	Importance	Effectiveness	Gap
Create a climate of caring and support for adults.			
Create a climate of caring and support for students.			
Provide a safe environment for teaching and learning to occur.			
Provide professional support through instructional guidance.			
Provide professional materials to enhance the instructional program.			
Provide the gift of time.			
Allocate money for professional resources.			

ship practices regarding the leadership strength of creating a climate of caring and support. Again, school councils and school staffs can use the same approach, modifying the key points as they see fit, to gather data about their own responsibilities for supporting this crucial ingredient of resilient schools.

You, as a school leader, can conduct your own informal feedback session by asking yourself these questions:

INFORMAL REFLECTION BY SCHOOL LEADERS

- ♦ To what extent have I created a climate of caring and support for adults?
- ♦ In what ways have I created a climate of caring and support for students?
- ♦ How have I provided a safe environment for teaching and learning to occur?
- ♦ How have I provided professional support through instructional guidance?
- ♦ In what ways have I provided professional materials to enhance the instructional program?
- ♦ To what extent have I provided the gift of time?
- ♦ To what extent have I allocated money for professional resources to support our priorities?

5

Take Charge!

School leaders, by definition, are take-charge people. They possess a certain circuitry that sends messages to their brain to raise their hand and say, "I volunteer to lead the charge." The school leaders we refer to are not only the administrators in the school. As we emphasize throughout the book, school leaders can include teacher leaders, school councils, and even school staffs.

But why are we writing a chapter about taking charge if readers are already taking charge? Because the same circuitry that tells you to raise your hand and volunteer to lead the charge under so-called normal conditions may send you different messages during adversity. Your challenge—and the purpose of this chapter—is to strengthen the skills necessary to keep your hand up and volunteer to take charge when it is most necessary, during adversity. Specifically, we discuss the leadership skills required to:

- Recognize the difference between taking charge under normal conditions and taking charge under adverse conditions.
- Assess conditions to determine when decisive action is needed.
- Act courageously on your convictions, in spite of the risks.
- View mistakes as another form of learning.

RECOGNIZE THE DIFFERENCE BETWEEN TAKING CHARGE UNDER NORMAL CONDITIONS AND TAKING CHARGE UNDER ADVERSE CONDITIONS

The assorted instruments that profile characteristics of leaders invariably include a dimension about being proactive. Successful leaders want to be in the spotlight, enjoy taking risks, have confidence in their ability to lead others, and follow through on their leadership charge.

Those who aren't wired to be take-charge individuals observe with a hint of envy others who seem naturally inclined to put themselves in the spotlight and publicly at risk of not delivering the goods. Leaders make leading look so effortless.

TAKING CHARGE UNDER NORMAL CONDITIONS

Taking charge under normal conditions is, for many people, rather effortless. These individuals have been honing their leadership traits since childhood. They are the ones who organized the neighborhood kids to sell Kool-Aid to sympathetic passersby. They are the ones who were selected to be student leaders of the school crossing guards. In high school, they were presidents of student government or captains of sports teams. And they are the ones who are now in leadership roles within schools. As one teacher leader describes her path to the teacher leader role:

> "I always liked being the leader and was sure that I wanted a career that maximized my skills. I took a long time to decide to enter education because I didn't see many opportunities for practicing leadership as an educator except maybe in the union. I was considering how I might get involved in politics or social causes. Then my aunt, a teacher, made me realize the role that a teacher leader can play in the school by getting involved in setting goals and instructional strategies, and that mentoring others is real leadership. Now, I'm working on my master's degree and looking ahead to becoming a principal."

So taking charge under normal conditions comes rather easily to this teacher leader.

TAKING CHARGE UNDER ADVERSITY

The rules change, however, when conditions of adversity are substituted for normal conditions. Under pressure conditions, leaders stare into a spotlight that may be a hot one, without any indication of when the light will go out. They face the possible consequences of leading in the wrong direction, which may yield disastrous results. In these high-stakes situations, leaders place in serious jeopardy a successful career as a leader. As the equation changes, so does the predictability of how leaders under normal conditions will perform under pressure. It is one thing to face familiar problems with tried-and-true strategies; it's a quite different thing to face an unknown situation without knowledge of what works, particularly when the stakes are high. As a veteran principal of an elementary school put it:

> "In order to be successful in the face of adversity, you need to anticipate adversity so it doesn't suddenly knock you down. What is the normal noise associated with change and friction versus what is something that is a little more dangerous? And you can't make the distinction without having the experience of dealing with both . . . and without having been burned. In other words: what's normal noise under normal conditions, what's growing legs of adversity, what do I need to pay attention to, and how do I know the difference? These are the questions you have to ask yourself."

Taking into consideration the principal's advice, notice how the concept of taking charge takes on a different character in the two scenarios below.

SCENARIO ONE

Jamie Maye Wilcox is principal of Newton County High School. She has served in this role for eight years, overseeing a growing student population that has strained the capacity of the school. Ms. Wilcox keeps a special file drawer for charts and graphs monitoring the student growth. For two years, she has been forced to improvise the use of school space in order to accommodate the enrollment bulge. Last year a multipurpose room became three classrooms. This year the faculty lounge and a testing area fell victim to the same fate.

As Ms. Wilcox reviews the numbers for next year, she painfully concludes that drastic action is needed. She knows, beyond a reasonable doubt, that the district needs a second high school. She notes with a twinge of sadness that this means she will lose some of her favorite teachers to the "other" high school. In all likelihood, she may also lose the state football championship trophy that graces center stage in the trophy case.

However, she also knows that instruction is beginning to suffer because too many students are herded into too small a space. Faculty morale is beginning to dip because of lack of space for creative work, for materials, for students to move around comfortably in classrooms. Too much instructional time is being lost as teachers move to other classrooms or jockey for space for their students. It's time to act and Ms. Wilcox exercises the same take-charge leadership skills that have been her trademark throughout her career. She schedules a meeting with the superintendent and school board president to review the numbers and present a solid case for a new high school.

SCENARIO TWO

Jamie Maye Wilcox is principal of Newton County High School. She has served in this role for eight years, overseeing a staff of eighty teachers. In fact, Ms. Wilcox will show you the charts in her file drawer pointing out the fact that she personally has hired over half the teachers.

One of the teachers, Mr. Lawrence, was her first hire, and she speaks with pride about how she took a risk by "rescuing" Mr. Lawrence, who had no prior experience in the field of education. He was laid off from his engineering job. He appeared on the doorsteps of Newton County High School, asking for help and saying he wanted to fulfill his dream of making a difference in the lives of young people. And for eight years he has done that, with glowing marks as a science teacher. Student achievement scores have risen in science and Mr. Lawrence recently established an Advanced Placement (AP) biology course. The students, parents, and community are very proud of the school's achievements in science, including the three first-place ribbons from the recent statewide science fair.

Mr. Lawrence also has reason to be proud for accomplishments outside the classroom. As athletic director, Mr. Lawrence points with pride to the new trophy case that is home to five state championship trophies, all won since he took over as athletic director. And, from a financial perspective, Mr. Lawrence has overseen the athletic booster club's fund-raising, now with an incredible balance of almost $300,000.

In leaving behind his engineering career, Mr. Lawrence also gave up a high salary and potentially attractive retirement package. After eight years of teaching at Newton County, Mr. Lawrence is within two years of being vested in the state retirement system. He says he can patch together his partial engineering retirement program with his teaching retirement program and achieve a modest retirement income. Because of personal health issues, this patchwork solution is critical to Mr. Lawrence in the future. And he likely won't be able to work more than two additional years.

But this scenario is really about today. Today, Ms. Wilcox sits at her desk with the door closed and the phone calls put on hold. She is meeting with a financial auditor, who hands her the report she requested. Over the past six months, more than $25,000 from the athletic department has mysteriously disappeared. The only person having access to the account is Mr. Lawrence. He collects the funds. He deposits the funds. He is the only one who can authorize expenditure of funds. Although there is not hard evidence pointing to what happened to the funds, there is a suspicious transaction involving the purchase of bleachers from a company owned by Mr. Lawrence's nephew. Mr. Lawrence is a partner in this company.

Ms. Wilcox reads the report again. There is no mistake. A large amount of money is unaccounted for. Mr. Lawrence is definitely involved in his nephew's company. The auditor's report offers substantial evidence of Mr. Lawrence's entanglement with the missing money.

There is also no mistake about Mr. Lawrence's financial and health condition. He desperately needs two more years of teaching or it will spell financial ruin for him. If he loses his job, he also loses health insurance coverage.

Finally, there is no mistake about the professional and personal risks to Ms. Wilcox of investigating a popular teacher, when there is no "hard" evidence implicating him in any wrongdoing.

Ms. Wilcox has at least two choices. In light of the report, she can choose to monitor the situation and hope for the best. Or Ms. Wilcox can pick up the phone and call the school board attorney, setting in motion a chain of events with the predictable outcome of "mess and stress" stamped all over them and her.

Ms. Wilcox knows that others know she took a risk and "rescued" Mr. Lawrence in the first place. Indeed he has exceeded all expectations when it comes to his professional role. Ms. Wilcox begins to rationalize why she can monitor the situation and take no action at the current time:

> "After all, the primary goal of our school is to raise student learning and Mr. Lawrence has certainly done that. Look how much our test scores have gone up! There would be a negative impact to losing Mr. Lawrence for the students. He's just started the AP program and the students love it. We just won some new respect for our science program with the blue ribbons. And look at the success of our sports programs! Who could fault me for monitoring the situation and not acting impulsively?"

Now, that's a pretty sound argument. If student achievement is the primary focus of a school, then doesn't it make sense to protect those who deliver it? Under normal conditions, the answer is yes. But this is not an ordinary situation, certainly not one Ms. Wilcox was ever trained to handle.

Ms. Wilcox stands up and begins to pace her office. She weighs the options, considers what matters most to her and her school. She then returns to her desk, dials the school board attorney's number, and gets a recorded message that the attorney is out of town until next week.

Ms. Wilcox hangs up the phone and wonders if this is a sign that she should take a wait-and-see attitude.

ASSESS CONDITIONS TO DETERMINE WHEN DECISIVE ACTION IS NEEDED

These scenarios underscore the point that clear-cut guidelines for taking decisive action under normal conditions become rather murky when it comes to taking decisive action in the face of adversity.

To help bring some clarity to the issue, we propose that school leaders apply the following benchmarks to help recognize when it is time to act on an issue.

IS WHAT MATTERS MOST TO US IN JEOPARDY?

As we discussed in previous chapters, first and foremost you need to be clear on your core values. If you are able to articulate what your school stands for among the values competing for your attention, you can make your decision in the light of what matters most. Once you are clear on this, you also have a clearer perspective on whether or not you need to act. If core values are in jeopardy, then it's time to do something and do it now.

In the scenario involving Mr. Lawrence, ethical values related to honesty and "right and wrong" conduct were called into question. These ethical values take precedence in the core values hierarchy over values related to an individual's impact on student learning.

In summary, be proactive and take decisive steps in the face of adversity when core values are at stake.

UNDER WHAT CONDITIONS WILL THE ISSUE GO AWAY?

It's human nature to want to believe that the issue will just go away and leave you alone. Some school leaders revert to the non-leadership strategy of waiting and hoping—waiting for signs the issue will disappear and hoping for the best.

A more risky and, at the same time, more courageous strategy is to actually identify the conditions under which the issue will go away. Beginning the question with "under what conditions" causes you to consider the *possible* conditions that could make the issue disappear. The companion step is to determine the probability that the conditions you listed will indeed occur. If the chances are low that the necessary conditions will actually materialize to make the issue go away, then it's time for action.

Mr. Juarez, principal at Kennedy Elementary School, told us about an issue he faced the first year after he was transferred to Kennedy, and how he watched to see if the issue would just go away. In general, he had heard reports from the previous principal that Mrs. Tipp was a weak teacher. Specifically, he had heard in the fall that many students in Mrs. Tipp's first grade classroom were unable to read beyond the pre-primer level, but he decided to reserve judgment until he could observe for himself. At the end of the year when reading scores were used for determining placement for second grade, Mrs. Tipp's students' reading scores were far below those of the other first grade teachers, and the children in the other classrooms came from similar backgrounds to those in Mrs. Tipp's room. Mr. Juarez began to think about next steps, the long hours of observation necessary to document Mrs. Tipp's poor teaching, and the potential union action if he were perceived as harassing her. Since Mrs. Tipp had been teaching for twenty-two years, Mr. Juarez rationalized she might retire soon. So he decided to wait and let time take care of the issue.

Five years later, Mrs. Tipp was still at Kennedy. And Mr. Juarez was still waiting. In our conversation, Mr. Juarez elaborated on what he learned from this experience:

> "Sometimes principals take the tack that maybe parents or teachers won't bring the problems to us. Or maybe they [the problems] will go away. That's what I did in Mrs. Tipp's situation. I just assumed—probably more accurately *wished*—that she would retire. But I didn't demonstrate the courage to confront the basic issue."

If Mr. Juarez had asked the question "Under what conditions will she retire soon?" he would have been obligated to consider very specifically the dynamics under which the issue would go away. Then, after he had articulated these dynamics, he would have had the data to objectively discern the probability of these dynamics occurring. In other words, what are the chances that the forces necessary to dissolve the issue will actually materialize? If the chances are slim that the problem will go away on its own, then Mr. Juarez has solid information supporting his decision that it is time to act.

WHAT ARE THE WORST-CASE OUTCOMES OF IGNORING THE ISSUE?

By ignoring the issue, at least in the short run you are granting permission for the issue to continue unabated. As the issue festers, what are the worst-case products of the festering? One of the high school principals in our study discussed the dangers that develop when issues fester:

> "When you have an issue, and the issue festers, you get more issues. And the more issues that develop, the greater the possibility that these issues will be divisive and cast a negative tone on the staff. If you deal with the issues when they come up, and you can either find a way to address it, diffuse it, or get another perspective, it helps to reduce the magnitude of the issue. There's less chance for fallout."

If the issue can literally produce results that are harmful to people, programs, and what matters most to your school, you have an ethical obligation to act. You can't afford to run the risk of serious harm by not acting. By asking what the worst-case outcomes might be, you force yourself to consider what might happen if you don't take charge.

WHAT ARE THE BEST-CASE OUTCOMES OF ACTING ON THE ISSUE?

Sometimes school leaders get so caught up in agonizing over the possible worst-case outcomes of making a wrong decision, they lose sight of the positive perspective. You can turn this around by considering the best-case outcomes. If you act on the issue, what are the most positive things that can come out of your action? As you make the list, you will see rather vividly that people and the system can benefit from the actions you take. And these positive elements will also help you see that inaction prevents the positive elements from ever seeing the light of day.

If you are willing to take action to make the best-case outcomes happen despite adverse conditions, you send a powerful message to those watching you. You are willing to take significant risks to make good things happen for your organization. You also model for others the risk taking that you expect as part of your organizational culture. A teacher leader in an urban middle school talks about the take-charge attitude that permeates his school:

> "One thing we do here is that as soon as we see a problem, we are on top of it. When we get a call from a parent, then we're there, physically there, or on the phone. I have been in houses at 11 at night, looking for a student. When you find them you have a conversation explaining, '"I am here *now* because I care about you and your school work."'

Notice that taking charge in the above scenario is part of a schoolwide culture. Teachers could choose not to be looking for students at 11 P.M. But, by acting on the issue immediately, the teachers know that good things will come from their actions.

So the message is clear: act and give the best-case outcomes a chance of being realized, even in the face of adversity.

ACT COURAGEOUSLY ON YOUR CONVICTIONS, IN SPITE OF THE RISKS

When you are faced with deciding whether to take action as a leader, at least three questions create an interactive dynamic that influences how you internally work through the relationship between the magnitude of the issue and the courage of your convictions.

WHAT ARE THE ODDS THAT I WILL FAIL?

None of us wants to set ourself up for failure. Particularly in leadership roles, failure is not part of an admirable track record. So you understandably weigh the odds of failure versus success before you act.

WHAT'S AT STAKE IF I FAIL?

If you fail to win the lottery, you may have two dollars at stake. If you fail to invest wisely, a lot more money is at stake. And if you fail to improve student achievement, a lot more than money is at stake. By being clear on what you're placing at risk of losing if you fail, you can more clearly assess if the risk is worth it.

WHAT ARE THE VALUES THAT ARE AFFECTED BY MY DECISION?

Philosophically, be clear on the values you want to achieve through your decision to act. As discussed throughout this book, under normal conditions when the risk of failure is low and when the stakes are low if you do fail, then it's rather easy to take charge. For example, let's suppose the chair of the school's parent–teacher organization invites you to help raise funds at the school festival by walking a balance beam. She tells you that the balance beam is eight feet long, eight inches wide, and eight inches from the ground. Do you have the courage to step up to the beam and contribute to the financial success of the school festival?

You mentally respond to the questions posed above in the following way: There's not much chance of my failing. If I do fail to walk the beam, aside from some lighthearted teasing, I don't have much at stake. And if I do walk the beam successfully, then I achieve the value of helping to support the school.

So, it's a no-brainer, right? You walk the plank.

Suppose, instead, the chair of the school's parent organization tells you the balance beam is eighteen feet long, eight inches wide, and eighteen feet from the ground? Do you eagerly step up to the beam and contribute? Probably not.

So what has changed? The level of risk has been raised considerably. And now, at such a height, the stakes of failing are higher. Your safety could be in jeopardy. So what is driving your decision is a high risk of failure, high stakes if you fail, and rather insignificant values—raising funds—if you succeed. If you decline to walk the plank, most people would understand and respect your decision.

Now suppose you are on a hike with your son and you encounter a slippery homemade bridge spanning a river below. Your son goes first, slips on some moss, and is clutching the edge of the bridge as rapids roar beneath him. You are faced with walking this eighteen-foot bridge, eight inches wide, with a steep drop to the rushing water eighteen feet below.

Again, a no-brainer, right? Because of the values affected by your decision, you decide to walk even as you subject yourself to risky conditions.

In the day-to-day pressures of school leaders trying to decide whether or not to take decisive action in a given situation, these same dynamics come into play. To help you work through these dynamics, we suggest you start with question number three: "What are the values that are affected by my decision?"

First and foremost, you need to be clear about the values at stake in your decision to act. If the values embodied in the issue are bedrock values that are important to you as a school leader, then our strong recommendation is to be true to your values, irrespective of what you risk by failing and irrespective of the odds of success. If you don't act on the values that matter most to you, then you end up falling into the proverbial trap of being event-driven, not value-driven. And those whom you are leading can detect event-driven actions in a heartbeat. So, if the values are important, you must act on the courage of your convictions, even at the risk of failure.

Second, if the values driving the decision are not crucial values, if you have a lot at stake by failing, such as wasted energy and frustration, and if the odds are rather low that you will achieve your goal, then perhaps the best decision is not to act. The resilience account of your staff can't absorb very many withdrawals on the account balance, if what you are pursuing is rather unimportant and you have a rather low probability of success.

In summary, if you want to strengthen the resilience of your school, focus the school's energy on those results that are most important, anchored in a clear understanding of why the results are worth the effort.

VIEW MISTAKES AS ANOTHER FORM OF LEARNING

No matter how good you are, the law of averages (and the fact that you are human) predicts that you are going to make mistakes. And take-charge people probably make more mistakes than others because they take more risks. Yet, those who take more risks, intelligent risks, are the real leaders among us.

One of the risks you take is not knowing all the answers. Some people placed in leadership roles don't take risks unless they know the answers, unambiguously, in advance. They don't volunteer to field-test a new mathematics program that the district is considering. They don't offer perspectives on controversial issues unless they have a reading on what the superintendent considers to be the "right" answer.

Resilient leaders do speak up, even when the "right" answer is unknown, because they've considered the issue and know how it relates to what matters in their schools. They are not inflammatory in presenting their ideas. But they take the risk of speaking, even without knowing what the boss thinks is important, because they know what values they hold dear. And have you ever noticed whom the boss calls for when there are tough decisions to be made and the answer is unknown? It's often the individuals who speak up, based on a set of core values, even if their actions are considered politically incorrect. And even if their actions turn out to be a mistake.

Furthermore, resilient leaders are quick to acknowledge their mistakes, make the necessary adjustments, and move ahead.

Mistakes just mean that risks are taken, that something new is tried. When the staff sees you make mistakes, they see that they have the same permission to be courageous and risk making mistakes. They are free to experiment, to try out an idea, and if it doesn't work, it's not a disaster. Resilient schools know they will take risks and have failures, and they also know they will live to see another day; few decisions are irrevocable. An elementary principal we interviewed for this book said it this way:

> "It doesn't bother me if I screw up big-time to say so. I will be the first to tell people. It's important for people to understand that I make big messes. Rarely is it something that can't be fixed by somebody. Even if it is in concrete, it can be pulled out quickly. You see, wet concrete covers nicely!"

What a powerful message! Wet concrete covers nicely. This principal is communicating very clearly to her staff that student learning is the school's priority. Through conversations with teachers in the building, we also learned that when the principal listens to a teacher describe a problem, her first question is likely to be "What have you tried to solve the problem?" She asks the question in a non-judgmental way that implies nothing beyond her expectation that the teacher has tried, or at least considered, possible solutions. Staff members are not afraid to tell her what didn't work because she's modeled for them that it's okay to make mistakes.

As stated at the beginning of the chapter, our plea to take charge is not meant to convey that the principal should take charge personally over all actions of the school. We intend to convey throughout the book that taking action is a collective responsibility of administrators, teacher leaders, and school staff. One other caveat: The leadership strategy of developing and implementing approaches to progress in the face of adversity does *not* mean blindly plowing ahead. As we discuss more fully in chapter 6, on flexibility, we are talking about moving ahead with all of your senses on full alert to adjustments needed along the way. With the leadership strategies presented in this chapter, you should be well on your way to taking charge of what's needed to advance student success.

COLLECT FORMAL AND INFORMAL FEEDBACK ABOUT LEADERSHIP TO TAKE CHARGE

The leadership strategy of taking charge includes the step of taking charge to collect feedback about the congruence between leadership values and implementation of these values. Fig. 5.1 provides you a feedback inventory to gather data on this topic. As a school leader, you will find the data helpful about how you can improve in this area. School site councils and school staff also will find the inventory form a useful tool for their own growth in creating a take-charge culture.

On a more informal basis, consider examining the questions below as a basis for your own reflection.

INFORMAL REFLECTION BY SCHOOL LEADERS

- In what circumstances have I recognized when action was needed and acted quickly?
- To what extent have I checked to see whether what matters most to me is in jeopardy?
- In what ways have I assessed the conditions under which an issue would go away?
- How have I examined the worst-case outcomes of ignoring an issue?
- How have I assessed the best-case outcomes of acting on an issue?
- To what extent have I assessed the odds of failure when faced with acting on an issue?
- To what extent have I assessed what's at stake if failure occurs when acting on an issue?
- How have I analyzed the values that were affected by my decision to act?
- In what ways have I viewed mistakes as another form of learning?

FIGURE 5.1 FEEDBACK INVENTORY ON TAKING CHARGE

Instructions: For each key point, record your rating on a 1–5 scale. To indicate the level of *importance* you attribute to each key point, record the rating in the *Importance* column.

1	2	3	4	5
not important		somewhat important		highly important

To indicate the extent to which the key point has been *effectively implemented*, record the rating in the *Effectiveness* column.

1	2	3	4	5
not implemented		somewhat implemented		highly implemented

Compare the ratings to determine the *gap* between importance and effectiveness.

Key Point	Importance	Effectiveness	Gap
Recognize when action is needed and act quickly.			
Recognize when what matters most to me is in jeopardy.			
Assess under what conditions the issue will go away.			
Determine the worst-case outcomes of ignoring the issue.			
Determine the best-case outcomes of acting on the issue.			
Assess the odds of failure.			
Assess what's at stake if failure occurs.			
Act courageously on my convictions.			
Analyze the values affected by the decision.			
View mistakes as just another form of learning.			

6

Remain Flexible in How You Get There

Most schools can point with pride to the ways they have been flexible in the past. They managed to adjust to changes in enrollment. They voluntarily agreed to change their strategies for grading students. Or they decided to change their approach to teaching reading. However, a school's resilience capacity is tested to the limit when it must demonstrate flexibility under imposed change. In this chapter we present leadership strategies to help you and your school:

- Know the difference between external change and internal transition.
- Recover quickly from setbacks.
- Develop skills to help you be flexible during Tweener Time.
- Learn to work within imposed constraints.
- Seek diverse perspectives.

KNOW THE DIFFERENCE BETWEEN EXTERNAL CHANGE AND INTERNAL TRANSITION

In this section, we draw on the work of William Bridges regarding organizational change (see, for instance, his books *The Way of Transition* and *Managing Transitions*) and Jerry Patterson's writings on school change (*The Anguish of Leadership* and *Coming Clean about Organizational Change*) to amplify the differences between change and transition. We also discuss how school leaders can work with staff members to effectively move through the phases of transition.

THE COMPLEX WORLD OF CHANGE

Many times you may understandably use the terms *change* and *transition* interchangeably. However, they are two distinct constructs and each plays a role in how you respond, flexibly or inflexibly, to imposed adversity.

Change is an external event that happens to you. Change can be sudden or it can evolve over time, but, either way, change disrupts the status quo. Change is also a complex construct because of built-in paradoxes. Paradox one: If you want to protect what you have, you have to be willing to change. In other words, if you want to protect what you care about most in the long term, you have to be willing to be flexible and change how you get there. Whether the topic is long-term personal relationships or long-range professional goals, a refusal to flexibly adjust strategies in the short term virtually assures defeat of what matters most in the long term.

For example, assume you get an unexpected call from a former colleague in another state. She is now superintendent of schools in one of the most respected school districts in the state, about a three-hour drive from your house. She offers you a position as assistant superintendent for instruction, an assignment that would dramatically advance your chances of securing your five-year goal of landing a superintendent's position. You couldn't have written the script any better for your professional advancement.

The downside is that your wife has just been accepted into a Ph.D. program at the local university. Your daughter will be a senior next year, and you have elderly parents in failing health who live in the community. You are faced with the paradox of changing in order not to change. Translated, you may need to change your professional goals in order not to change what matters most to you, support for your family.

A second paradox relates to changes over time. Isn't it curious that the very things you want to safeguard from changing are themselves the products of change? And the status quo that you are fighting to protect was, sometime in your history, just as daunting a change as those changes being imposed on you now. As Bridges (2001, pp. 1, 2) points out, "No matter how solid and comfortable and necessary the *status quo* feels today, it was once new, untried and uncomfortable. Change is not only the path ahead, but it is also the path behind us, the one we traveled along to wherever we are trying to stay."

So change happens. A retiring superintendent. Another reorganization. A new state mandate. But it is not the external change per se that undermines your resilience. It's the human transitions that can do you in.

THE PARTICULAR POWER OF TRANSITION

Transition is the human process we all go through internally to make sense of the external changes done to us. Transition is the way we make sense out of the event.

Take, for example, the school board's announcement of a new superintendent in your district. A school board meeting is called and, in front of a packed house, the school board votes to hire someone from another region of the country as superintendent. After the vote, board members close their notebooks and leave the room, and they leave you, the high school principal, with the heavy duty of managing the transition at the school level. The event, a change in superintendents, is over. The human transition of working through the event has just begun. And how you lead the staff through the transition dramatically affects the resilience quotient of the school.

In order to help your staff make the necessary internal transition in response to external change events, you need first to know about the two phases of transition leading to your acceptance of the change. Next, you need to apply this knowledge to develop strategies that help your staff (as well as yourself) be flexible in moving through the transition process. In the following paragraphs we offer a brief explanation of the two phases of transition. In subsequent sections, we develop more fully the specific strategies necessary to help you move through the transition process in a healthy way.

THE TRANSITION PHASE OF ENDINGS

As paradoxical as it seems, all changes designed to produce something new must begin with letting go of the old. In other words, all new beginnings begin with the transition phase called Endings. Note that there is a distinction between the decision to end something and the human process of working through the external change. The event, such as a school board decision, is the external change. The process that you and the staff go through to make sense of the event is the transition phase of Endings.

With the change in superintendents, you may lose security, connections, predictability, or friendships. Any one of these losses can negatively affect your resilience. In combination, these losses can take a huge toll on your capacity to move ahead in the face of the change.

THE TRANSITION PHASE OF TWEENER TIME

Once you come to terms with the reality that every new transition process begins with Endings, you face the reality of the second phase, Tweener Time. Tweener Time is the ambiguous, in-between period that occurs after you leave the safe harbor of the past and before you have any glimpse of what the new shore looks like or exactly where it is located. At first, Tweener Time feels like unbridled chaos, when you are adrift with no sign of port.

Given the power of this phase to completely deplete your resilience account on the one hand and, on the other hand, to give you a resilience-building boost, it is imperative to understand Tweener Time. As a school leader, if you don't anticipate this phase and understand its power to set you back or move you ahead, you're likely to push your staff swiftly through it without taking the time necessary to move ahead constructively. Remember, this phase is a natural and important part of adapting to adverse changes. It can't be rushed.

In addition, if you underestimate the power of Tweener Time, you will likely try to skip over it and hop directly to the so-called new beginning. One school district attempting to implement major central office reorganization called us and asked us to do a two-hour workshop on transition. When we suggested that the organization's staff might need more than two hours (how about two months) to work through Endings and Tweener Time, the district reorganizers responded, "The staff are all grown-up people. They need to act like adults and get a life and get on the with reorganization."

Needless to say, there was not a match between what the district officials wanted and what we thought they needed. So they did the two-hour version with internal "facilitators." And six months later, the district was adrift. They tried to skip over Tweener Time and their resilience account paid the price in the long run.

After Tweener Time has been successfully negotiated, you will begin to get an actual glimpse of the distant shore. When this happens, people move from flickering images of what the change may bring to clear pictures of something concrete. Even though the picture may be fuzzy at first, as you catch the wind and build speed, the intended objective becomes clearer and more believable. Because you have been flexible in applying strategies to move you through the transition phases of Endings and Tweener Time, you arrive at your new "destination" with your resilience intact. Such an experience builds your capacity to strike out again when the new becomes the old and it's time to let go yet again.

To review the central message in this section: School leaders need to be clear about the differences between externally imposed changes and internally created transitions. Leaders also need to have a strong grasp of the components of transition. Finally, school leaders need to be able to apply strategies to help their staffs remain flexible as they move through the phases of transition. In the next section, we outline essential strategies to achieve flexibility in the face of adversity.

RECOVER QUICKLY FROM SETBACKS

Adversity happens. You can't wish it or will it away. So when a setback does happen to your organization, you have two basic choices. You can choose to act surprised and wallow in the victim role. Or you can accept the setback as reality and move on. Our advice to you is straightforward: Don't spend your resilience points being surprised or pretending the setback doesn't exist. Instead, spend your resilience points figuring what you can do to recover quickly.

Recently a school leader invited a speaker to spend a day at the school exploring the theme of moving ahead in the face of adversity. As the day unfolded, the speaker kept hammering on the theme that schools need to let go of the "poor me" syndrome and start facing up to the changes that are so vitally needed in education. In not-so-subtle words, the speaker sent the school staff a stiff message to get on with their life of implementing change.

Finally, one seasoned teacher raised her hand and hesitantly asked, "But given everything that's been imposed on us in the past two years, isn't it all right if we take a little time to lick our wounds?"

Her point is right on target. Whenever you face setbacks, it is perfectly natural (and healthy) for you to move through the customary stages of grieving, including denial, anger, depression, bargaining, and grudging acceptance. In fact, it is unhealthy in the long run to attempt to skip over the grieving process and move directly to the new life after the loss. The key to flexibility in the face of adversity is how long you spend licking your wounds. Understandably, with issues as grave as death or other tragedy, the grieving cycle is longer. When it comes to the less traumatic setbacks your school faces, such as budget cuts, retiring staff, or changes in programs, the faster you can bounce back, the quicker you can refocus on your passion for student learning. The following examples illustrate the point.

CONTRASTING RESPONSES TO IMPOSED SETBACKS

Hanover Middle School and McAdory Middle School in the Susquehanna School District were informed last March by the school board that there would be a freeze on new hires because of budget problems. Schools would not be able to fill vacancies in teaching assignments and would have to "make do" with existing resources.

Not surprisingly, both the Hanover and the McAdory staffs reacted emotionally to the decision handed down by the school board. They were disappointed by their lack of involvement in the decision and, more importantly, they were worried about the impact that larger class sizes would have on the quality of student learning. For a period of time, both schools spent their resilience points on disappointment and worry. A fundamental difference was the length of time the two schools stayed stuck in their own grieving.

Hanover School staff couldn't seem to get out of the victim role. They rallied parents to protest the hiring freeze. They appeared in front of the school board with petitions for lifting the freeze. As the school year progressed, their energy shifted away from the new programs Hanover had recently initiated to the point where these programs were put on the back burner as the staff continued to protest the freeze.

In contrast, the McAdory staff reluctantly came to terms with the reality that the hiring freeze wasn't going to go away in the near future. So the staff directed their energy to the question "Given the reality that the hiring freeze is with us for a while, how can we spend our energy in constructive ways to help our students achieve?"

By framing the question in "how can we" terms, the McAdory staff moved away from the victim role, recovered from the setback, and proceeded to use their resilience points in a constructive way. For example, the school found ways to use some of its professional support staff to work directly with the classes having the most needy students, in effect reducing the class size for part of the day. The staff also increased their efforts to find volunteer tutors in the community to work directly with students needing additional assistance. While the Hanover staff attended board meetings in protest, the McAdory staff attended the meetings of local civic clubs to solicit more volunteers. This is a clear demonstration of how a school can suffer the setback, feel the pain, and then move on to refocus on what is most important.

QUESTIONS FOR LEADERS TO CONSIDER DURING THE ENDINGS PHASE

According to William Bridges's research on organizations in transition, the single biggest reason that organizational change produces dysfunctional human transition is that leaders fail to pay attention to the endings and loss. He poses the following questions that all leaders should ask in order to help staff be flexible as they move through the Endings phase of transition (Bridges, 1991, pp. 32, 33).

- ♦ Have I studied the change carefully and identified who is likely to lose what—including what I myself am likely to lose?
- ♦ Have I been able to identify with the subjective losses individuals feel, even though I personally don't feel the losses in the same way?
- ♦ Have I given people the time and space to grieve over the endings?
- ♦ Have I given people accurate communication about the external change that is happening?
- ♦ Have I found ways to support people as they give up

part of their past, and found ways to let them take part
of the past with them?

♦ Have I helped the staff see that being flexible in moving through the change will actually help them be more
resilient as they keep in mind what is most important?

Asking and responding to these reflective questions about your
leadership role during the period of Endings will positively position you and your staff as you enter Tweener Time.

DEVELOP SKILLS TO HELP YOU BE
FLEXIBLE DURING TWEENER TIME

Drawing on the points made in chapter 1, at any given time
your school has a certain resilience capacity. This capacity remains
unaffected as long as conditions are running rather smoothly in
your school. However, for many schools, the resilience capacity
starts to shrink as conditions inside and outside the school become
more confusing. When the superintendent's office starts sending
mixed messages about the direction the district is heading, when
the school board votes to get rid of social promotion, or when the
state legislature says it is going to start giving schools a report-card
grade, conditions change from running smoothly to running amok.

In order to strengthen resilience when conditions run amok,
as a school leader you need to develop specific leadership skills
to help your staff respond in a flexible way to Tweener Time.

DEVELOP A HIGH TOLERANCE FOR AMBIGUITY

Recent research on the topic of tolerance for ambiguity looks
at "the extent to which individuals are threatened by or have difficulty coping with situations that are ambiguous, where change
occurs rapidly or unpredictably, where information is inadequate
or unclear, or where complexity exists" (Whetten and Cameron,
1993, p. 54). Research has found that individuals who have a high
tolerance for ambiguity are more adaptable and flexible under
ambiguous conditions than those who are less tolerant of change.
Whetten and Cameron report the following findings from admin-
istering the Tolerance for Ambiguity Scale: "In general, the more
tolerant people are of novelty, complexity and insolubility (problems that are difficult to solve), the more likely they are to succeed

as managers in information-rich, ambiguous environments" (Whetten and Cameron, 1993, p. 55).

In short, as a school leader under the pressure of adversity, demonstrate your tolerance for ambiguity. This advice was reinforced during a recent school visit associated with our resilience research. In this case, the designated teacher leader, a very organized physics teacher who likes everything planned well in advance, talked about the ongoing need for personally tolerating ambiguity in facing schedule changes.

> "You can't ever really know what will happen and you have to be ready for that. When the schedule here keeps changing right up to the last minute, we just laugh. I tell the teachers why the changes are occurring if I know and that helps. Some of them want to know if' [the change] is going to work. I can't give them any guarantees because I don't know. We all have to get used to being flexible about trying new things."

If ambiguity occurred infrequently in your personal and professional life, it might not merit much attention relative to resilience. However, as you can likely attest, ambiguity is rampant in all phases of your life. Just when you think you have conditions under control, something unexpected happens to throw more ambiguity your way.

So the first step in dealing with ambiguity is to acknowledge that it is not going to go away, at least not for very long. By shifting your thinking from "if only ambiguity would go away" to "given the harsh reality that ambiguity is going to hang around," you can embrace the reality of ambiguity rather than deny its existence.

This step of acknowledgment is a huge breakthrough in strengthening resilience. Recall the numerous occasions when you have heard your colleagues lament, "Why are things so confusing? Where are we heading, anyway? How in the world can we abandon what we've been doing when we don't know precisely what things are going to look like on the other end?" When this questioning starts, your resilience account starts to shrink because you wallow unproductively in worrying about why things aren't clear. Instead, increase your resilience by accepting the omnipresence of ambiguity. Imagine how liberating it is when you can say the following without a hit on your resilience: "Ambiguity, in one form or another, is going to be a rather constant force in the life of our school. Ambiguity is a reality that I need to work through or work around in order to stay focused on what matters most in this school. Ambiguity isn't bad, it just *is*."

Once you come to terms with the constant company of ambiguity, you need to model for others how to handle it. And make no mistake about it: your staff is watching to see how you react to even the smallest changes. If issues such as the schedule changes discussed above ruffle your feathers, then the message you send staff is that it's okay to be upset by the little things. If, on the other hand, you model a high tolerance for ambiguity, then the staff picks up on this message just as strongly.

PROTECT YOUR STAFF FROM FURTHER CHANGES

Your bottom-line challenge in Tweener Time is to lead your staff through the dark tunnel of ambiguity so they come out the other end healthy and productive. One way to accomplish this is to protect your staff as much as possible from further changes while they are struggling with the uncertainty of Tweener Time. The following vignette illustrates the point.

At Taurus Middle School, the principal and staff are excited about the peer-tutoring program recently adopted by the school. From the principal's perspective, this program holds promise for both the struggling students and the high school students who will serve as tutors. The school staff are poised to introduce the program at a parent meeting scheduled for Wednesday night.

On the previous Monday, however, the school board dropped the bombshell that all middle schools in the district must implement mandated character education programs within three months. The principal at Taurus realizes that the staff's resilience will take a nosedive if one more reform is added to their plate. The principal also realizes that the character education program is not going to go away in the short run, because two board members campaigned hard for this during school board elections.

Reluctantly and grudgingly, the Taurus principal announces to the staff that the peer-tutoring program will have to be put on "hold" during the board's big push for character education As the principal explains to the staff: "I know that you are going to spend a lot of resilience points trying to accommodate the recent board mandate on character education. And I know your plate already is overflowing. Therefore, I propose that we declare a temporary moratorium on our peer-tutoring program, until we work through this other stuff. You have my commitment that we will shift our energy back to this important initiative, once we work through the ambiguity of figuring out where the board is going with character education. But we need to make sure we keep the number of changes affecting you at any one time to a manageable number."

In summary, as a school leader you have a broad perspective on the various initiatives hitting the staff at any given time. You also have the authority to put a hold on certain initiatives until the staff safely navigates Tweener Time on the most pressing issues facing them. By acting as a buffer, you can influence staff resilience for the long haul.

CREATE A TRANSITION MONITORING TEAM

During periods of significant change, particularly during Tweener Time, schools need to be flexible in how they respond to the needs of the staff. As Bridges reports in *Managing Transitions*, leaders usually assume that all the feedback they need to help guide the staff through ambiguity will come through regular channels of communication. Bridges argues, however, that this is seldom the case. Instead, he lobbies for a "Transition Monitoring Team" to help the school be more flexible in responding to staff needs during adversity. More specifically, Bridges proposes that you form an ad hoc team of seven to twelve people chosen from as wide a cross-section of the organization as possible. It should meet every week or so to take the pulse of the organization during Tweener Time. It has no decision-making power. Rather the purpose of the Transition Monitoring Team is to facilitate communication so the organization can respond flexibly to questions such as these:

- How are things going for people during this ambiguous period?
- What are the rumors through the grapevine that need to be addressed?
- What do the leaders need to know that will make the transition period less chaotic for the staff?

Finally, Bridges advises that the Transition Monitoring Team needs to report frequently to the staff on visible, tangible steps taken to address concerns that have been raised. Once Tweener

Time is behind you, the Transition Monitoring Team can be put behind you, too. Make sure from the beginning that the team has a planned ending. Otherwise, with the best of intentions, you can create one more committee that drags on long after its purpose has been fulfilled.

SUSPEND THE RULES AND BE CREATIVE

Use the ambiguity of Tweener Time as a period where people can suspend the rules and be creative. Encourage staff to look for innovative ways they can use their time and resources to move ahead.

As one school district faces the ambiguity of yet another attempt at central office reorganization, the central office staff wonder aloud what the superintendent is up to this time. At the meeting called to introduce her idea, she comments, "I am proposing to abandon the well-entrenched district practice of central office subject-area specialists and, instead, to implement curriculum generalists in each school attendance area. I must acknowledge at the outset that I don't know exactly what the new model will look like. I do know, however, that we need to provide schools with less top-down subject-area supervision and more broad-based support in instructional practices."

Then, recognizing the need to suspend the rules and be creative, she adds, "During this period of letting go of the old model and struggling to figure out what the new model will look like, I strongly encourage each attendance area to seize the opportunity to design ways you would like to see central office resources structured to best meet your instructional needs at the school level. We will experiment with various models across attendance areas for the next eighteen months, then we will reach consensus on the model that best suits our overall needs."

The superintendent demonstrated several important skills in strengthening staff resilience. She acknowledged that she didn't have all the answers. She encouraged staff to suspend the rules and be creative. Finally, she didn't cast the staff into permanent Tweener Time. She specified a time frame for the ambiguity and experimentation.

PROVIDE TRAINING AND SUPPORT FOR STAFF

When adversity hits, be flexible in marshaling resources to address the concerns of staff. For instance, reorder professional development priorities to make sure staff members feel confident with their skills to work through the ambiguity of Tweener Time. In the central office reorganization scenario described above, the superintendent demonstrated flexibility by moving funds into the travel budget so individuals could visit other sites that have the new model in place. She also encouraged them to attend workshops and conferences to learn about strategies to make the proposed reorganization a reality.

In circumstances when you as a school leader are faced with Tweener Time, move beyond the *I Can't* tendency and instead initiate the *How Can I* strategy. Specifically, "How can I make Tweener Time, this interim period between the old and the new, not only a tolerable time but a time during which we can seize the energy of ambiguity to come out on the other end in a place that's better than where we've been?"

LEARN TO WORK WITHIN
IMPOSED CONSTRAINTS

For most of us, the resilience-draining acts that are hardest to cope with are those that are *imposed* by outside forces. On December 1, Lurleen Callaway faced just this problem when she was called to the Forest Park School District Board meeting. As the leader of a 300-student elementary school in the rural part of the county, she couldn't imagine why the board president had asked her to attend. She soon found out. The board had just voted to close her small rural school and merge students and staff with a larger school in a nearby suburban community. They decided that she would replace the much-loved retiring principal of the suburban school. They did not ask her what she thought of the decision or its impact on the programs of the two schools; "just do it," they said.

Because Ms. Callaway is a resilience-building leader, she knew there were key steps to be taken as soon as possible. After a restless night, she came to these conclusions about what to do next to act within the constraints imposed by the school board:

- Figure out exactly how teachers' behavior and attitudes will have to change to make the merger work.
- Determine who stands to lose something under the merger and find a way to help them deal with losses.
- "Sell" the problem that prompted the board to make the change.
- Find a way to help staff see the problems that led the board to make the change.
- Following the announcement to students, staff, and community, talk with people to see what kinds of problems they foresee with the merger. Involve them in solving the problems.
- Acknowledge that the merger won't be easy and talk about how people may feel during the transition.
- Immediately begin holding regular meetings with the merged staff to start building the new identity. Continue the meetings, perhaps even on a daily basis for only ten minutes, to help ease the transition when the new school year begins.

It's not surprising that Ms. Callaway successfully led the merger of the two schools. She didn't waste time moaning about what might have been, but she moved ahead to work effectively within the constraints imposed by the board.

SEEK DIVERSE PERSPECTIVES

If you are like most school leaders, you reached your current level of professional achievement by having a lot of right answers. You were rewarded in school for right answers, you were promoted through the ranks for having the "right" perspective, and now here you are in a leadership role, trained from childhood to be right.

Somewhere along this journey, however, most school leaders start to realize that there aren't many "one right answers." Somewhere along the journey you more fully appreciate the richness of diverse perspectives. Especially when adverse conditions happen, you find that it is in the collective best interest of the organization to actively seek perspectives different than your own. Indeed, to help other people be able to see diverse perspectives, you have to be open to different ways of thinking and let others see it in action. Here's Mr. Kirlyo's story.

Everyone in the school knew that Mr. Kirlyo had high expectations for students and teachers. They also knew that he was a kind man who would not tolerate humiliation or treating anyone with disrespect. He faced a personal dilemma when he had to move a teacher in the middle of the year because the teacher couldn't control his fifth grade class. He brought a second grade teacher into a fifth grade setting because he knew the teacher had high expectations for all students and their behavior. The very first day, the teacher told the students, "You are going to love me and you are going to hate me. But at the end of the year, you will be the smartest kids in the school and we are going to have a celebration." She posted a sheet on the classroom bulletin board that was titled "I Didn't Do My Homework Last Night." Mr. Kirlyo was surprised to see on the board the names of two students who had not completed their homework. He reflected on that seemingly minor experience:

> "Even though I didn't like that strategy, it worked. So I called the kids aside, and said I didn't like seeing their names there. And the kids didn't like it either. Normally, I wouldn't support this, but the class was out of control. This was a loving, caring person who had been teaching for eight years. So I had to be willing to see the situation from another perspective, to hold myself back and give her some latitude to use some strategies she felt would work. It was a tough class and she cleaned it up in a hurry."

It's important to remember that remaining flexible in how you solve a problem or confront an issue does not mean changing your core values. In fact, the reverse is true. If you are guided by core values as described in chapter 2, then you are open to a variety of ways to achieve your primary goals. Mr. Kirlyo didn't like the strategy used by the teacher, but he recognized that it was an approach that worked for her in bringing the classroom under control so that students could learn. His core value was to do whatever it takes to help students achieve academically and that value was not compromised.

In chapter 6, we have emphasized the distinction between external changes being done *to* schools and internal transitions being done *by* schools to move through imposed changes in a healthy way. We also have outlined concrete steps that school leaders can take to help schools maintain their resilience during the transition phases of Endings and Tweener Time. Based on our research with resilient schools, we have strong evidence that school leaders do indeed make a difference in supporting schools to remain flexible in the face of adversity, without giving up on their core values about what matters most.

COLLECT FORMAL AND INFORMAL FEEDBACK ABOUT LEADERSHIP TO REMAIN FLEXIBLE

The leadership strategy of remaining flexible becomes particularly important as school leaders collect information about their own leadership and then demonstrate flexibility as they adjust their leadership strategies in response to the feedback. Fig. 6.1 allows you to use the Feedback Inventory to assess how you are doing relative to remaining flexible in tough times. As we have underscored previously, school site councils and school staffs also should consider how they could benefit from assessing their own contributions to remaining flexible.

Finally, you can informally assess your contribution to being flexible through examining the questions below.

INFORMAL REFLECTION BY SCHOOL LEADERS

- ◆ How have I helped staff understand the difference between external changes we can't control and internal transitions we can control?
- ◆ In what ways have I helped staff recover quickly from setbacks?
- ◆ To what extent have I developed a high tolerance for ambiguity?
- ◆ How have I protected the staff from further changes during loss and ambiguity?
- ◆ How have I created ways to monitor our transition activities during periods of imposed change?
- ◆ In what ways have I suspended the rules and encouraged staff to be creative during the transition phase of ambiguity?
- ◆ To what extent have I provided training and support for staff during the phases of transition?

FIGURE 6.1 FEEDBACK INVENTORY ON REMAINING FLEXIBLE

Instructions: For each key point, record your rating on a 1–5 scale. To indicate the level of *importance* you attribute to each key point, record the rating in the *Importance* column.

1	2	3	4	5
not important		somewhat important		highly important

To indicate the extent to which the key point has been *effectively implemented,* record the rating in the *Effectiveness* column.

1	2	3	4	5
not implemented		somewhat implemented		highly implemented

Compare the ratings to determine the *gap* between importance and effectiveness.

Key Point	Importance	Effectiveness	Gap
Understand the difference between external change and internal transition.			
Recover quickly from setbacks.			
Develop a high tolerance for ambiguity.			
Protect my staff from further changes during loss and ambiguity.			
During periods of significant change, create ways to monitor transition.			
Suspend the rules and be creative during the phase of ambiguity.			
Provide training and support for staff during the phases of transition.			
Learn how to work within imposed constraints.			
Consider diverse perspectives.			

- In what ways have I helped the staff continue to work effectively within imposed constraints?
- To what extent have I considered diverse perspectives during adversity?

7

Be Positive in Spite of Adversity

School leaders enter their first leadership assignment ready to save the world, or at least the organizational unit that they are leading. Their resilience tank is full to the brim and they have energy to burn. But something happens along the way. Their internal catalytic converter takes the energy to burn and converts it to burnout. In more pragmatic language, the cumulative impact of encounters with adversity pushes many school leaders over the line from optimist to pessimist. And there are plenty of legitimate reasons for school leaders like you to be pessimistic about today's conditions in education.

On the other end of the spectrum sits a group of school leaders who proudly wear their rose-colored glasses. The tinted glasses come in handy to intensify the beauty of a sunset. When they are worn to work, however, they distort reality and negatively affect the long-term resilience of the wearers. The negative effect occurs because reality over time just can't measure up to the imaginary world the school leader perceives through the rose-colored glasses.

Somewhere between the extremes of perennial pessimism and unbridled optimism is the well-researched field of positive thinking. This chapter draws on the research by presenting specific strategies to help school leaders strengthen their ability to:

- Expect the world to be filled with disruptions.
- Anticipate disruptions whenever possible.
- See opportunities rather than obstacles.
- Think "how can we" rather than "we can't."
- Find humor in the midst of adversity.
- See the payoff at the end.
- Model a positive attitude.

EXPECT THE WORLD TO BE
FILLED WITH DISRUPTIONS

As a school leader it's not the surprises that negatively affect your resilience account. It's when you are surprised you're surprised. You can probably recall your first year on the job as a new school leader. You were relieved to just finish the year with your job and sanity intact. You may even remember uttering these familiar words, "The next year should be a normal one. No disruptions. No surprises."

When the disruptions and surprises returned in year two and wouldn't seem to go away, how did it affect your resilience? As we work with school leaders across the nation and around the world, we find that how they handle the disruptions directly affects their outlook, positive or negative.

A CASE STUDY ABOUT UNANTICIPATED DISRUPTIONS

Lu Len serves as principal of a central-city school in the heart of an Asian community in Los Angeles. She accepted this assignment after seven years as teacher and administrator in an affluent suburb of Los Angeles. During her time in the affluent district, she became accustomed to the resource base and the work ethic of the students. But she wanted to make a difference in the lives of students who were struggling, so she enthusiastically took on the challenges of her current assignment. Her outlook for the future was bright and positive.

Within her first six months as principal, she weathered student violence, student protests, budget cuts, state-imposed testing, and more. When she met with her supervisor to review her annual goals and action plan, she faced the reality of virtually no progress. And her outlook on the future took an abrupt U-turn from positive to negative.

Even though her evaluation conference lasted over two hours, her one-sentence summary captures her explanation for no progress. "I could have done what I set out to do if my school had not been afflicted with so many unanticipated disruptions."

When Ms. Len met with her mentor a week later and recounted the conference, particularly her complaints about the disruptions to her plans, the mentor cut to the heart of the matter:"Welcome to the real world of this community. The disruptions you've experienced aren't going to go away. They will just change names and shapes. If you hope to salvage a positive outlook in this assignment, you only have one choice. Expect the future to be filled with disruptions to your expectations. Build this expectation into your framework for making sense of the world you work in. Then take your annual goals and pose the challenge, "How can I move ahead on these goals in the face of disruptions that will inevitably occur?"

MOVE BEYOND THE DISRUPTION

Let's apply the mentor's message to your own circumstances by first restating a harsh reality: Disruptions to your expectations will happen. Even though you long for predictably stable conditions in your leadership role, the only predictability you can count on is the predictability of disruption. If you continue to deny this reality, you will continue to be surprised and disappointed when disruption rears its ugly head again. And the surprise and disappointment take their toll on your resilience account.

If, on the other hand, you expect the world to be filled with disruptions, when the disruption does indeed hit you in the face, you aren't knocked down by the punch. You don't drain your resilience tank by moaning that you could be more positive if only disruptions left you alone. Instead, you recast your thinking in a positive mold by acknowledging the reality: "Disruptions happen." This orientation to disruptions helps you make sense of the world and its apparent surprises and, correspondingly, gives you strength to move beyond the disruptions.

Along with the strength to move ahead, you need to approach disruptions with this question in mind: "Given the recent disruptions to our progress, what will it take for us to move ahead?"

One school leader we interviewed described how he thinks about disruptions: "You get immune to surprises. You may not be able to predict exactly what will happen, but a real *surprise* seldom happens."

In summary, if you view the disruptions as the natural result of the changing world we live in, you have a greater chance of being positive about the overall condition of things. You don't waste resilience points worrying about the disruption. Instead you treat disruption as reality and work your way to a positive outcome.

ANTICIPATE DISRUPTIONS WHENEVER POSSIBLE

The previous section argued that you can strengthen your positive outlook by expecting the world to be filled with disruptions you can't predict. A companion resilience-building strategy is to anticipate disruptions whenever you can. To illustrate this principle, let's return to the example involving Ms. Len. As a first-year principal, her inexperience contributed to her being surprised by disruptions that she couldn't predict. However, let's fast-forward to two years later. With a couple of years under her belt, Ms. Len is now in a better position to anticipate, based on the wisdom of experience, potential problems associated with budget cuts. So she is better able to help the staff stay positive because she can anticipate the disruptions and develop contingency plans in case budget funds dry up again.

Recall, in your own leadership experience, when you have anticipated possible disruptions and developed contingency plans to deal with the possible disruptions. Recall as well the impact on your resilience account, knowing that you were vigilant about what *could* happen and feeling prepared to deal with the disruption.

A combination of an anticipatory outlook and contingency planning helps to plug any holes in the resilience reservoir inflicted by potential disruptions.

SEE OPPORTUNITIES RATHER THAN OBSTACLES

You have probably participated in optical illusion exercises like the one where you look at a drawing and you are asked to describe what you see. Some people see an old lady. Others see a young maiden. The so-called reality of the drawing doesn't change. The filters people apply in their interpretation of the reality affect how they *see* the reality out there.

THERE'S GOT TO BE A PONY IN HERE SOMEWHERE!

To illustrate the point another way, we share the story of two young brothers. One brother was a very sad and unhappy little boy who cried continually and just didn't know how to be happy.

The other little boy was always happy, no matter what happened to him. The boys' parents were concerned about the extremes in the behavior of the children and decided to consult a psychologist.

The psychologist prepared two rooms for the boys. The sad child was placed in a room filled with his favorite toys, cake, ice cream, balloons and everything the psychologist believed would delight a child. The parents and psychologist observed the child through a two-way window as he hung his head and sobbed uncontrollably.

The second child, the happy one, was placed in a room piled high with manure. They watched as he dug happily through the pile. When they asked the child why he was so happy digging in manure, he replied, "with all this (manure), I just KNOW there's got to be a pony in here somewhere!"

FIND OPPORTUNITIES WITHIN IMPOSED MANDATES

In a similar way, how school leaders and their schools interpret the reality of changes happening *to* them affects how positive (or negative) they are in light of the changes. Facing the same reality, some people see messes that they have to clean up and some believe there's got be a pony in there somewhere.

For example, state-imposed report cards for schools are not a figment of the imagination. The requirement is something tangible and real that 'has been imposed in many states. It will not go away, at least in the short run. So you can't change the reality through denial, whining, or wishing it would go away.

What you *can* change is how you as a school leader view the change. Your point of view in turn shapes how your staff views the imposed change. Do you see the report card as fraught with problems? For instance, the report card could be used to pit one school against another. It could cause the legislature to reduce funding in schools that receive "bad" marks. The report card could cause parents to flee low-scoring schools in favor of schools who make the grade.

Or do you see the report card as an opening, an opportunity to advance the efforts your school has already been working on? For example, the report card can become a benchmark to guide how you modify your curriculum to conform more closely to state expectations. It can be another way to demonstrate publicly that your school is making the grade in the face of adversity. It can influence parents to choose to stay in your community because there is "objective" evidence that you all are performing at least as well as neighboring districts.

If you look for the pony, you will find it. One of the teacher leaders from an urban high school put it this way: "There's always something good going on and we try not to dwell on the bad things. Kids are going to be kids and they're going to get into messes. But we believe you find what you look for. If teachers expect kids to fail or get into trouble, they will. It's that simple."

DON'T DENY THE OBSTACLES

We need to emphasize that seeing opportunities instead of obstacles does not equal denying the obstacles. It does not mean donning the rose-colored glasses so your perception of reality is distorted. To help you stay positive, we recommend that you describe the reality of the change you are facing. Then participate in a discussion with your staff about the obstacles. The "yeah, but—" response is natural and you actually drain staff resilience by trying to totally squelch it. In fact, as we discuss in more depth elsewhere in the book, by acknowledging the negative side of the equation, it frees you up to let go of the baggage associated with the obstacles. Now you are in a position to use your energy positively to move ahead by acting on the opportunities awaiting you.

THINK "HOW CAN WE" RATHER THAN "WE CAN'T"

One major piece of wisdom we have gleaned from our work with resilient schools is summarized by a poster hanging in an assistant principal's office: "It's not so much what you do, it's how you think about what you do that makes all the difference."

AVOID THE VICTIM ROLE

When life erects formidable barriers right in front of us, the natural tendency is to respond with an outlook of "I can't get over it." The same tendency applies to our life in schools. When schools encounter adversity, in whatever form, they frequently assume the victim role of "We can't." The victim role is much more comfortable because it lets you avoid responsibility for both acknowledging the circumstances and, more importantly, acting on the circumstances. As long as your school says, "We can't do what we need to because of all of the adversity we face," you escape any accountability for your own school's actions. Imagine the school leader who tells the community, "We can't put computers in all of our classrooms because the district won't give us the money to do it."

CREATE POSSIBILITIES WITH *HOW CAN WE* THINKING

Imagine, instead, the school leader who asks, "How can we work with you as community leaders to find creative funding sources that will allow us to reach the goal of putting computers in all of our classrooms?" Shifting your thinking from "We can't" to "How can we" creates a more positive scenario than lamenting that you can't because of your adverse circumstances.

In one school we visited recently, the teacher leader described what it's like to take the "how can we be better than we ever imagined?" approach in a school that no one expected to succeed:

> "We've been recognized three times for being an exemplary school. Exemplary means that all your reading, writing, and math scores are above 90 percent. In 1999–2000, we were named a national Blue Ribbon School. We're 80–90 percent Hispanic, free and reduced lunch, and it's almost like people expect our children and teachers to fail. We're proud of what we've done."

If you, as a school leader, allow your school to paint the barriers erected in front of you with *we can't* brushstrokes, you're going to paint your school into the victim corner. Translated, as long as your school responds to adversity with "We can't," then you have no room to move, no choice but to fail.

In contrast, if you paint the same circumstances with the broad brush of *how can we*, you create possibilities. It's just a matter of how you do it. Figuring out how to do what you need to do is a much more uplifting, positive set of tasks than automatically assuming you can't do it.

Consider the situation one school found itself in when the State Department of Education (SDE) unexpectedly, at midyear, decided that bilingual students would have to take the standardized achievement test. Many schools were caught off-guard because they'd assumed these students would be exempt as usual.

At Socrates Middle School, a seventh grade bilingual teacher had twenty-two or twenty-three students who he thought were going to have another year to have a practice achievement test before taking the real one. Because of the SDE ruling, his students suddenly were forced to take the real test and have their scores included in the school average.

The teacher leader stepped in and decided she was not going to let this teacher and students experience failure just because these children weren't yet ready for the test. She vowed, "We'll get them ready." She helped the teacher totally reorganize his classroom. Other teachers took the students judged most likely to do well on the upcoming test, so that the bilingual teacher could work with a smaller group. Then the staff helped him come up with a way of organizing even smaller groups within his classroom so that he could do Spanish with one half of the class and English with the other. That strategy allowed him to work with those students who needed more time just to get comfortable with the language.

The teacher leader proudly reported to us the outcome of the school's responding to the bilingual teacher's need for help:

> "We thought it was going to be a real setback for us because it was so unexpected. But the way my colleagues and I helped him out made a difference. And we made it to exemplary status just like the year before."

To reiterate the message on the poster in the assistant principal's office: "It's not so much what you do. It's how you think about what you do that makes all the difference." The simple shift in language from "we can't" to "how can we" symbolizes a complex shift in thinking that will help you and the organization you lead stay more positive and, in turn, more resilient.

FIND HUMOR IN THE MIDST OF ADVERSITY

Of course, laughter is good medicine. And of course it is natural to find stuff to laugh about when things are going your way. On the other hand, finding humor in the midst of adversity feels more like an unnatural act.

So our recommendation to you is this: act unnatural. Do whatever it takes to find humor in the thick of your adverse conditions. The research both in psychology and physiology documents positive effects from exercising humor during tough times. Gail Sheehy, author of the best-selling book *Pathfinders*, reports that the ability to see humor in a situation is one of the four coping strategies that people who overcome life's crises use as protection against uncertainty and change.

Humor is also important because it helps create bonding. Laughter is the same across all cultures. We don't have to speak the same language to share laughter. It is a universal form of communication that most of us are comfortable with and enjoy. You've probably experienced the relief that comes when someone in the room cracks a joke during a tense situation. The humor breaks the tension of the moment and the bond of laughter pulls us closer together.

Another important learning from our research is that conscious demonstration of a sense of humor by school leaders has a calming effect on staff. Leaders who demonstrate a sense of humor give a sense of power over conditions that they can't control or change. It's as though those circumstances that are causing distress and pain are somehow minimized when leaders laugh about them and draw others into that laughter. A teacher in a suburban middle school described the impact of humor as used by her principal: "The principal has an incredibly strong sense of humor and a very stress-free type of management. He makes us laugh just about every day. That leads to a positive environment in a place where you have a lot of change."

As we talked with people in resilient schools, we realized that humor can be found in several contexts: humor in the absurd, humor in the predictably ridiculous, and humor in our own actions.

FIND HUMOR IN ABSURDITY

In your role as school leader, can you recall times when you and your organization received a directive from above that made absolutely no sense? The actions being demanded offered no positive benefit for students or adults. The actions had no connection to the current direction you were heading in. And the actions showed no other positive payoff. Under such circumstances, you face two choices: You can "cry" about it, or you can laugh about it. If you choose to cry, you can devote months to gnashing your teeth, writing memos to central administration, and complaining to staff about the absurdity of the latest dictate. If you choose to laugh—and remember it is a choice—then you minimize the negative power of the dictate and create the energy to move forward.

We are not talking about laughing at people as human beings. We are talking about being able to see the absurdity of the situation and realize that you can't even begin to find a "pony" in the mess. Finding humor in the ridiculous helps you put it in perspective. You and your colleagues face many adverse challenges that are much more serious in nature than the recent directive from above.

One school principal we interviewed talked at length about a state- legislated report card for schools. The report cards keep score on student achievement in five core areas. So each school receives five grades that are averaged to arrive at an overall school score. The major newspapers in the state publish all of these scores for each school.

The state legislature also decided that any school scoring below average in any area needs repair and will be forced to develop a school improvement plan to bring the school up to at least the midpoint of the scale. The school improvement plans must be funded from the local district budget. No state funds are set aside to help the "below average" schools.

One more point: The legislature decided that the measures used for the core areas should not be criterion-referenced measures; they must be norm-referenced. In effect, this state legislature crafted a policy that declares that in any given subject area half of the schools in the state are broken and in need of remediation. And they must develop improvement plans to remediate, even if their performance level shows 80 percent mastery in the subject area.

So the state will automatically have half the schools needing remediation in every subject area every year. The public will see the results and understandably form impressions of a failing system.

Absurd? Yes. Can you find any humor here? You have to. You can't make sense of it, mathematically or logically. You can't fight it in the short run. So your challenge as school leader is to help the staff find humor in the ridiculous and move on with what matters most to you.

FIND HUMOR IN PREDICTABLE PATTERNS

As we discussed previously, one ingredient in staying positive is to expect disruptions and not be surprised by them. For instance, let's suppose your superintendent belongs to a national superintendents' network that convenes a high-powered conference each summer. Each fall, your superintendent returns with a truckload of new programs. Each year she begins her "Welcome Back" workshop with a new program that lands in your lap at the school level.

So each year when the teachers take their seats for your own "Welcome Back" session, the standard line is "What new program did the superintendent hand off to you this time?" The teachers have come to expect a recurring pattern of "adopt the superintendent's newest fad." As a staff you can flail, grouse, whine, and pout. But in the end you are going to have to show some visible sign of compliance. Your challenge as school leader is to help the staff find the humor in the predictable pattern and, most important, find ways to link the newest event to the ongoing efforts your school is making to stay focused.

BE ABLE TO LAUGH AT YOURSELF

Standard advice to new administrators is "Take your job seriously and take yourself lightly." Great in theory but tough to practice. Particularly if you are a school leader who has not been seasoned by experience, each new challenge seems to be more of a test of your ability to keep your job. So when you screw up, the natural reaction is to become even more worried about how your staff and supervisor view your competence. Then you become even more serious and any sense of humor you brought to the job evaporates.

In a recent interview, one teacher leader told us the story of her "transformation" from lighthearted teacher to serious teacher leader:

> "I was selected by the teachers in my school to fill the newly created position of teacher leader. The job description called for me to provide support and guidance to my colleagues in the areas of best instructional practices and cutting-edge curriculum. Having served in the school for

thirteen years, I brought to the position a strong sense of the school's history and a strong base of respect from my colleagues.

But something happened along the way. Soon after I changed from teacher to teacher leader, I also changed (in my own mind) from a lighthearted teacher to a serious, purposeful administrator. I started making unilateral decisions. I started bossing my former colleagues around, telling them what they could and could not do. I was a serious, self-appointed supervisor.

After about two months, two of my close professional colleagues invited me to beverages after school at one of our favorite hangouts. Following about thirty minutes of chitchat, my colleagues shifted to business. They told me in no uncertain terms about my change in conduct. "'We didn't select you to be teacher leader so you could become teacher boss. We selected you because you have the skills and respect from colleagues to support us in the vision our school has embraced for the past ten years. You're beginning to alienate your support base. It looks to us like you have two choices. You can be a teacher leader in our school or you can be a teacher boss somewhere else. And we tell you this because we care about you and also want you to be successful in your new assignment.'"

What a wake-up call. I went home that night and didn't sleep a wink. I wrestled with their comments, at first denying to myself any truth in what they said. As I became more reflective, I started seeing in my mind examples of where I did indeed act as a self-appointed boss of my teacher colleagues."

The next afternoon, we had a regularly scheduled faculty meeting and I asked the principal if I could have about fifteen minutes at the beginning of the agenda. Looking a little puzzled at my ambiguous request, he agreed.

I came to the meeting wearing a baseball cap the staff gave me when I first took the job. Across the front of the cap were the words "Teacher Leader." Addressing my colleagues, I thanked them again for the cap I was proudly wearing. Then I told them, "'I didn't realize that the cap you gave me was a magic cap."' I turned the cap 180 degrees on my head and presented the audience with a new "front" of the cap with the words "Teacher Boss" across the front. At first there was stunned silence in the room. Then the silence turned to tentative snickers, then outright laughter.

I explained to the staff that during my first six weeks on the job the cap magically turned from being a Teacher Leader cap to a Teacher Boss cap. But because I was wearing it, I couldn't see it turn. They were the only ones who could see it. And I went on to point out that it took the courage of a couple of teachers in the room to make me take off the cap and confront the words '"Teacher Boss."' I reassured my colleagues that I still wanted the job of Teacher Leader and if, at any time, they saw my hat turn, they needed to tell me about it because, otherwise, I might be the last to know.

By creating an environment of being able to laugh at myself in the face of the adversity created by my self-appointed job, we all were able to laugh at the situation and, more importantly, I could laugh at myself. This freed us to move ahead in the direction we all wanted in the first place."

Relating the above experience to your own world, recall times in your job as school leader when you made mistakes and took yourself so seriously that everyone suffered. In general, if you can step back from the immediate crisis and ask yourself "What was it that I messed up on about six months ago?" you will be hard pressed to produce an answer. Whatever it was that concerned you is now history and you learned from it and moved on.

Taking cues from the teacher leader's "Teacher Boss" story, when you start taking yourself so seriously that it has adverse effects on your colleagues, seek ways to laugh at yourself in the face of adversity. The laughter helps put things in perspective for you and those around you.

SEE THE PAYOFF AT THE END

Whether you are a marathon runner or a cancer patient or a school leader, in order to help you stay positive in the midst of adversity, you have to believe that what you are going through at the moment is worth the reward at the end. You will endure short-term pain for long-term gain. When school leaders work with staff on a preferred future for their school, by definition the target is a long way off and the journey will be a long one. Along the way, the bumps, detours, and apparent dead-ends are enough to cause the fainthearted to turn around. Even for the believers on the journey, setbacks can evoke discouragement, second-guessing, and a negative climate.

REMEMBER *WHY* YOU ARE ON THE JOURNEY

As a school leader you can contribute to a positive outlook by helping people remember why they signed up for the journey in the first place. When Dave Tarmak assumed the principalship at Acton High School, he also assumed responsibility for turning around Acton's ten-year reputation as a poor performer. He and the school embarked on a five-year plan to have all students performing at least at grade level.

During the journey setbacks inevitably occurred. The popular assistant principal resigned for health reasons. School mobility increased. The local newspaper had a penchant for pointing out what was wrong at the moment, rather than seeing the progress made over time. In the face of all of this, Mr. Tarmak relentlessly refused to let the distractions deter him. He constantly reminded staff and students to recall what life was like in the school five years ago. It was not a pretty picture to recall. He consistently talked about the best-case outcomes of having all students perform at grade level. In other words, even in the middle of the pain of the moment, Mr. Tarmak supported a positive environment through his vigilant attention to the payoff at the end.

KEEP YOUR EYES ON THE PRIZE

In another example of this same theme, an elementary school teacher leader talked to us about her commitment to high academic success for children in the low-income school where she worked:

"I have a strong belief that I can make an important difference in the life of a child from this low-income area. The parents love their children, they care, and they want a better life for their children, but they don't always know how to do it. Sometimes, they're working so hard to feed their children that they can't help a lot at home with reading or math. When I see kids come to us very low academically and see them exit this school at their scoring level, I know that I have given them the opportunity to be what they want to be. What they choose to do with it is up to them. But they leave with the skills to be successful. I am rewarded in that way. And our community is a better place."

Admittedly, even the stouthearted can lose sight of the payoff during the daily grind. It is possible to know there is a long-term payoff and still get frustrated with daily annoyances. Yet, those who are able to refocus even on the bad days find that remembering the payoff can help build resilience

MODEL A POSITIVE ATTITUDE

Not surprisingly, school staff members watch every move a school leader makes, searching for cues about what things are really like. If you think this opening statement isn't true, consider what you know about your supervisor. You may know the model of vehicle she drives, as well as personal information about family or friends, and you can probably tell when she is angry, disappointed, or about to praise you. In a similar way, your staff watches you for cues. Is our school really in trouble? What is *your* reaction to the school board election? Will the bond referendum pass?

So if the staff is watching you for cues, what cues are you sending and to what extent are you even aware that you model what you want in others? One teacher leader in an urban high school told us he is extremely aware of the impact of his attitude on others:

"I lead by example. I don't complain. I just go with it. I keep a positive attitude and let others see it. A negative attitude by a school leader is like a virus. Once it starts, everyone complains of the same symptoms. Then all of a sudden everyone feels unhappy and whining and complaining about everything. So, if it never starts, we can use that energy to "just do it." Everyone stays up that way instead of allowing one person to bring everyone else down."

From the daily interactions with people in the hallways to the ongoing interactions about the future health of the school, modeling positive leadership is prerequisite to positive attitudes by staff and students. We especially admire the perspective of a middle school principal in a particularly tough urban area. We referred to him in another chapter and the steps he took to clear gang activity out of his school. He explained his view on the value of a positive attitude like this:

> "To help with the positive attitude, I walk in the door and put a smile on my face and speak to all of the teachers. Even if it has been a horrible day and I'm feeling rough on the inside, I convey an upbeat attitude with staff. Even if I am tired and exhausted, I stay upbeat. Because if the staff sees me wearing down, then it affects them. I walk the hallways all day to show energy."

Successful, resilient school leaders also capitalize on positive attitudes of others in the school. A classroom teacher or cluster of teachers on a particular grade level who demonstrate a positive attitude and belief that they make a difference can become persuasive to others without a word being spoken. A high school principal noted the impact of veteran teachers' attitudes on their colleagues:

> "A big success of the school is the people who have been here since the beginning. Through their attitudes and work habits other people see what we are trying to accomplish and they start to buy into it."

One final caution: Finding humor in adversity is hard work. As one wise principal advised us:

> "You don't just wake up all of sudden and have a sense of humor. You make a conscious effort to build the climate over time, to look at the ludicrous things with a sense of humor. You don't just do it once."

In closing, we want to emphasize once again that remaining positive in spite of adversity is a necessary prerequisite to building a resilient school. If teachers, students, and parents see that school leaders adopt a defeatist attitude, they will think it's okay for them to do the same. As a leader, your attitude is a mirror that reflects on the staff. In this chapter we have presented strategies for you to make the reflection a positive one.

COLLECT FORMAL AND INFORMAL FEEDBACK ABOUT LEADERSHIP TO BE POSITIVE IN SPITE OF ADVERSITY

By using the Feedback Inventory Form in fig. 7.1, you can formally gather information about the importance and effectiveness of your leadership strategies to help others, as well as yourself, continue to be positive in the face of adversity. Recall that you can adapt the key points listed in fig. 7.1 to match the values that you want to measure.

FIGURE 7.1 FEEDBACK INVENTORY ON BEING POSITIVE

Instructions: For each key point, record your rating on a 1–5 scale. To indicate the level of *importance* you attribute to each key point, record the rating in the *Importance* column.

1	2	3	4	5
not important		somewhat important		highly important

To indicate the extent to which the key point has been *effectively implemented,* record the rating in the *Effectiveness* column.

1	2	3	4	5
not implemented		somewhat implemented		highly implemented

Compare the ratings to determine the *gap* between importance and effectiveness.

Key Point	Importance	Effectiveness	Gap
Expect the world to be filled with disruptions I can't predict.			
Predict disruptions whenever possible.			
Seek opportunities instead of obstacles.			
Think "how can we?" rather than "we can't."			
Find humor in the midst of adversity.			
Seek the payoff at the end.			
Model a positive attitude.			

You can also informally gather similar data through self-reflection as you pose these questions:

INFORMAL REFLECTION BY SCHOOL LEADERS

- How have I handled disruptions to my expectations?
- To what extent have I anticipated disruptions and built contingency plans for them?
- In what ways have I seen opportunities instead of obstacles?
- To what extent have I modeled "how can we?" thinking rather than "we can't"?
- In what ways have I found humor in the midst of adversity?
- To what extent have I remained positive by focusing on the payoff at the end?
- How have I modeled a positive attitude?

8

Create Meaningful Participation and Shared Responsibility

Even under the best of conditions, school leaders sometimes feel overwhelmed by the responsibility for building a sense of community among students, staff, and community. For example, throughout the book we have emphasized that you as a school leader have a responsibility to help the school stay focused on core values, maintain high expectations, create a climate of caring and support, take charge as needed, remain flexible along the way, and stay positive.

The responsibility to achieve these goals doesn't rest with you alone. The responsibility should be shared among your staff and community. This is tough to accomplish under good conditions. During difficult times, building a sense of participation and shared responsibility among diverse interest groups becomes more challenging but more critical than ever. The purpose of this chapter is to outline strategies to increase your odds of strengthening participation and responsibility for the healthy future of your organization, even in the face of adversity. In particular, you will learn how to:

- Achieve meaningful participation.
- Achieve shared responsibility for decisions.
- Decide who decides how decisions get made.
- Develop consensus strategies based on core values.
- Encourage everyone to contributo.
- Acknowledge the presence of conflict and resolve it constructively.
- Make reasonable mistakes and admit it.
- Untangle compromise, consensus, and unanimous consent.
- Provide consensus-building training.

ACHIEVE MEANINGFUL PARTICIPATION AND SHARED RESPONSIBILITY FOR DECISIONS

Meaningful participation appears, on the surface, to be readily endorsed by everyone who gets to be involved, particularly those who were excluded from sharing under the more dictatorial models of the past. However, appearances can be deceiving. As we describe below, the actual practice of broad-based participation in schools sometimes produces a backlash effect, with teachers and other staff protesting that they didn't have time to be participating so much, to be doing the "leader's work." They were too busy teaching. Then, when you stir shared responsibility into the mix, the dynamics become even more complex. Finally, throw in a little (or a lot) of adversity, and "meaningful participation and shared responsibility in the face of adversity" becomes a recipe for disaster.

The topic of site-based management (SBM) has been hanging around for over thirty years. In one of the earlier interpretations of the concept, site-based management meant pushing the decision-making pyramid down to the school level. Instead of the top (district office administrators) telling the middle (principals) to tell the bottom (teachers) what to do, early versions of SBM meant that the top (principals) told the middle (teachers) to tell the bottom (students) what to do. The justification for this decision-making structure was linked to the effective schools research pointing to the need for strong leaders at the school level. As the argument goes, principals need to be take-charge people who are experts in curriculum and instruction. This expertise empowers them to direct teachers in best practices. As one principal said about his view of shared decision making in the "good old days": "Yeah I believed in shared decision making in the eighties. I made decisions and shared them with the staff."

In the 1990s, SBM began to shed the cloak of hierarchy and instead embraced a more inclusive model. School Improvement Teams (SITs) popped up everywhere, sometimes by choice and sometimes by legislation. These SITs were charged to produce SIPs (School Improvement Plans), again sometimes by choice and sometimes by legislation. When the smoke cleared from the production of SITs and SIPs, however, many schools still looked and acted the same as they had before.

Reflecting on the twisting path of site-based management through the halls and history of schools across the country, we begin to sense why the road has been so rocky. Many schools, school districts, and even legislatures operated, with the best of conditions, to create new structures and policies without first investing the time to seek staff perspective or to construct core values supporting the structural changes. So, for example, Plank High School formed a School Improvement Team, and the principal controlled the agenda and heavily influenced the outcome of the SIT's activities. The core value of meaningful participation never entered the picture.

One of the teacher leaders in our study described the introduction of school improvement planning in her school:

> "We began having all these after-school meetings to discuss school improvement without ever knowing what was wrong with things they way they were! We thought we were a pretty good staff and didn't understand why we had to waste so much time when we didn't see a reason! We felt like the principal had a hidden agenda and wouldn't tell us what he wanted. It was like a game and it was our job to figure out the right move."

So an essential step for school leaders committed to meaningful participation is to invest ample time, up front, in constructing core values about what the slogan *meaningful participation* truly means to staff. Later in this chapter we will outline in more detail what the process and product might look like.

For you as a school leader, articulating a value about meaningful participation is a necessary, but not sufficient, condition for deciding how your school will make decisions. To complete the cycle, you also need to confront the companion issue of shared responsibility for the decisions. It's one thing to participate in the decision-making process. It's quite a different matter to share in the responsibility, and therefore be held accountable, for the decision made. In the following sections we draw on the work of Jerry Patterson in *Leadership for Tomorrow's Schools* (1993) as we address the heavy-duty power question of "Who decides?" and the most power-riddled question of all: "Who decides who decides?"

DECIDE WHO DECIDES HOW
DECISIONS GET MADE

As we discussed in the various interpretations of site-based management, one way of deciding is for you, as school leader, to decide. Another way of deciding is not to actively decide. Failure to take action on an issue is, by default, a decision. A third approach to deciding is the more participatory approach of voting. Voting is the democratic way for most groups. It is efficient, generally non-confrontational, and simple to understand. All it takes is for you to call for the vote and count the "ayes" and "nays." The outcome becomes known immediately; the majority wins.

A relative newcomer to schools is the idea of deciding by consensus. Consensus means the group reaches a collective decision that virtually everyone can support. Although the slogan of consensus decision making offers inherent appeal, the process possesses its own set of problems. Later on, we explore in more depth the problems and how to overcome them.

In deciding how to resolve this issue of shared responsibility for the decisions, we return once again to our core values, particularly to the notion of opening up the system to more widespread involvement and ownership. Does your school truly believe that the power to make decisions and affect change should be distributed throughout the school? Do you believe that the collective expertise of the staff usually makes for wiser decisions than can be made by the solitary expert at the top of the organization chart? Do you believe that empowerment is most effective when people have access to the support, information, and resources to get the job done? In other words, what does your school truly believe about opening up the system to meaningful participation and shared responsibility? Constructing core values around these questions will inevitably lead you to the answers, which in turn will lead you to developing strategies and structures for putting the values in place.

A principal in a low socio-economic status (SES) school in a large urban area described her conversion to meaningful participation and shared responsibility as being driven by a desire to see students be successful. She said, "You can't make a difference as an autocrat and you can't do it alone." She added:

"You have to do it in steps and as a team. In the past I have been an addicted enabler. I have taken on the responsibilities that should have been moved to teachers. So I have had to make a shift from enabler to empowerer. I am still working on it, but there is no alternative."

In the above example, the principal spent many years making all of the decisions and enabling the staff to be free of responsibility for the climate of the school. Over time, she found that the strategy was not in the best interest of anyone, students or adults. So the principal had to learn the new role of empowering people with opportunities for participation and responsibility.

WHAT ISSUES DESERVE GROUP ATTENTION?

In arriving at an answer to the above question, schools need to be sensitive to the power and control trap. Not every single issue deserves group attention—but it is tempting and natural for individuals (including you as school leader) to see discussion on this statement as an opportunity to revert to the boss model. If you as supervisor control which decisions are eligible for group participation, you essentially have returned power to the top of the organizational chart. The same effect occurs if a School Improvement Council manipulates the system so that all group recommendations must be approved by the council before a decision is declared official.

If your school constructs a value saying that the school should involve all interested employees in discussing issues that affect their professional lives, almost any issue becomes fair game for group discussion and decision. As your school tries to operationalize the value, don't be surprised if it wants to declare all categories of decisions open for group resolution. For instance, one school insisted on everyone sitting together to debate every issue facing the school, including the flavors of soft drinks in the vending machines and grade of paper for the copying machines. As trust was built among the school staff and time became even more precious, the staff decided that the principal could handle some decisions and others could be assigned to the School Improvement Council.

In other words, group decision making does not translate automatically into the whole group making decisions on every issue that pops up. Routine items and issues arising from crisis adversity, for example, are that don't lend themselves to calling a group together for the decision. One teacher we interviewed pointed to the principal's handling of routine matters as a real bonus for the staff:

> "The administrative mumbo jumbo doesn't filter into the classroom. The principal takes most of the heat for administrative stuff and most of it never trickles down to the classroom."

The same teacher also recognized that convening a group to deal with a crisis is not realistic. She explained:

> "If it is irate parents, the media, etc., [the principal] will try to keep it away from the teachers; he protects us. As an example, we had a parent who came because her student was suspended. She was profane, and tried to enter the academic area. He kept her confined, had the custodian close the classroom doors so the students and teachers couldn't hear it. If that parent had gotten into the academic area and caused trouble, the whole day, academically, would have been ruined. In another case, we had some student bring marijuana to school and he intervened directly before it got to the staff."

Many times, however, schools do indeed apply a shared-responsibility model to create the decision-making tree for how to effectively and efficiently address crises when they arise. That practice builds trust. A teacher leader told us how her school's crisis plan worked with a real incident:

> "We had a couple of situations this week where we supposedly had a man with a gun out in the field over here firing in the air. We knew from the crisis planning what to do. The teachers went in to lockdown. We told all the kids to get under their desks, we pulled the blinds down, all the doors where locked and lights were out. I knew that our building was secure because I knew Mrs. Hoya, our assistant principal, had already secured the outside doors because I knew what had to be done and who would do it. I knew my principal would contact authorities and jump in front of somebody before the person could get to the office staff, the kids, or us. I had no fear. I was scared of

maybe somebody being hurt on the outside of the building, but I had no fear that the person was coming in here. That just isn't going to happen. If I were at some other schools where I've taught, I would have felt like it were just me against the world. That's not how it is here. We have a plan and everybody plays a part."

Even for categories of issues that are determined to be important for group consideration, not every group member has to participate in order to maintain group resilience. To mandate participation could be counter to the spirit of your core value. At Hawthorne Middle School, the staff adopted guidelines for participation saying that any individual may choose not to participate in the discussion of an issue; he or she may even elect not to attend the meeting scheduled for such discussion. Inserting this provision into the ground rules for group decision making honors the individual's judgment about the need to participate. It also honors the individual's judgment about having to choose among the priorities competing for the person's time and energy. And when this choice is extended to individuals, each individual's resilience account is strengthened.

Along with each individual's choice to decline participation on a particular issue comes the responsibility of you and the rest of the school staff not to play "gotcha" with the individual. In other words, colleagues should not sit in judgment of the person's choice, nor should they hold this against the person in future discussion. Part of establishing a consensus process is that an individual may "pass" on this round, this issue, but that doesn't mean he or she can't participate later on another issue.

At the same time, the right to choose carries a major responsibility for the person choosing. Specifically, if your physical education teacher, Mrs. Dagley, chooses to opt out of your group's decision about block scheduling, by default she endorses the decision and its implications for her professional assignment. Otherwise, "gotcha" gets played in reverse, if Mrs. Dagley tries to use her absence from the discussion as power to block the group's progress.

As long as your school clearly defines the ground rules for participation and balances the individual's right to opt out with the group's right to move ahead with a decision, surprises, power plays, and drains on resilience will be kept to a minimum.

HOW DOES YOUR SCHOOL MAKE GROUP DECISIONS?

Once your school decides, philosophically and procedurally, what issues deserve group attention, the next question is "How do we reach group decisions?" Two basic options are before you: your school can vote, or your school can reach consensus. As mentioned earlier in the chapter, voting has several virtues. It also presents a major drawback, depending on your school's core values. When majority wins, minority loses. And the minority that opposes the decision can be as much as 49 percent of those voting. The implications of voting reach far beyond the win-lose outcomes. The vote mentality leads to use whatever strategies are necessary to secure votes and this leads back to the power-and-control model for your school's decision making. If your school endorses meaningful participation and shared responsibility, you need to confront the reality that voting takes you in the opposite direction.

In the previous sections, we addressed several basic questions about meaningful participation and shared responsibility. There remain, however, some lingering clouds hanging over the meaning of consensus.

Ideally, the spirit of consensus means that you reach a collective decision everyone supports, after openly and extensively considering the many diverse aspects of the topic being discussed. Consensus is *not* finding the lowest common denominator of the group's ideas; it does not mean agreeing to the little piece of common ground found among the many, varied perspectives of your staff.

Consensus does mean seeking higher ground and creating a new solution that incorporates and, at the same time, goes beyond individual perspectives. Consensus decisions clearly illustrate that "all of us are smarter than any one of us."

DEVELOP CONSENSUS STRATEGIES BASED ON CORE VALUES

Achieving meaningful participation and shared responsibility, especially during adverse times, won't happen through shortcuts. The most direct path is to be clear about your values and develop your consensus strategies around the values. For example, one school we visited, Hague High School, had constructed the following core values:

- We value employees actively participating in any discussion or decision affecting them.
- We value diversity in perspectives that leads to an enriched knowledge base for decision making.
- We value employees resolving conflict in a constructive way, leading to stronger solutions for complex issues.
- We value employees reflecting on their own and others' thinking in order to reach better decisions.
- We value employees acknowledging mistakes and learning from them.

Below, we show how these values directly affect the consensus-building process.

ENCOURAGE BROAD PARTICIPATION

The strength of consensus decisions rests in part with school leaders encouraging everyone in the group to become serious contributors to the problem-solving process. But, as we have emphasized previously, participation is more than just talking. Consensus building requires that all participants in your school honor the right for each colleague to be heard without interruption, in an environment of trust and open communication. This calls for a commitment by each individual to be genuinely interested in what's being said.

SEEK DIVERSITY OF PERSPECTIVES

The consensus process expects everyone to listen to all points of view, acknowledging that even the most unpopular viewpoints deserve fair examination. In the old days of top-down decision making, diversity was seen as a deterrent to good decisions. If the school leader and staff disagreed on a topic, leaders were trained to convince the dissident voices to come around to the leader's way to thinking.

Based on the core value about diversity developed by Hague High School, the whole notion of diversity gets turned upside down. If you, as school leader, disagree with another's perspective, you have an ethical obligation to listen intently to the other perspective. You also have a similar obligation to learn *why* the "dissenting" voice is dissenting. Perhaps insights you glean will help in the formulation of a stronger decision. When all of your school staff think alike, not much is gleaned that will contribute to a rich collective decision.

RESOLVE CONFLICT CONSTRUCTIVELY

Most educators have been trained to avoid conflict in their professional lives, particularly when adversity brings conflict of its own. Traditional interpretations of conflict translated into the belief that conflict is bad; harmony is to be achieved at all costs. Conflict, as interpreted by Hague's values, incorporates conflict as an inevitable and potentially constructive way of school life. When the principal led Hague High School through a tough situation, he watched for signs of conflict. When he saw it, he moved toward the tension, not away from it. Conflict does indeed bring out deep differences in perspectives. It amplifies the diversity among group members and contains the yeast for a rich solution that helps move the school through the adversity to a positive outcome.

CREATE REFLECTION TIME FOR GROUPS

Without question, consensus building takes time. In fact, because of the time factor alone, some schools revert back to the old decision-making models of voting or letting the principal decide. Then they wonder what went wrong as their school cultures grapple with the shock waves from the old power-and-control thinking rather than shared-participation and shared-responsibility thinking.

Based on Hague High School's core value regarding reflection, they continue to search for ways to find reflective time for groups to deliberate important issues. Valuing reflective time in reaching consensus means valuing the time to talk things out until all serious objections to a unified course of action have been resolved. Consensus requires suspension of judgments and premature positioning. When you take positions and defend them zealously, you reduce the likelihood of reaching a group decision incorporating the best of individual perspectives. By creating reflective time for consensus building, the Hague staff helps assure that they achieve two fundamental goals of lasting decisions: a shared knowledge base and group ownership for the decision made.

BE OPEN TO MAKING MISTAKES

Consensus building occurs in an atmosphere that encourages people to think out loud about the universe of possibilities available for reaching a decision. As your school strays from the most logical solutions to those that have never been dreamed, you make yourselves vulnerable to sounding foolish. As an illustration, Hague staff members endorse a core value about mistakes that celebrates way-out thinking, along with the prospect of not having the right answer.

Similarly, consensus includes the possibility that the group decision could be wrong—or at least not the best possible solution. This belief becomes critical as you wrestle with what to do about those individuals who steadfastly disagree with the direction the vast majority of the group is heading in. As we discuss more fully in the next section, a group decision shouldn't be held hostage by one or two strongly dissenting voices. At the same time, openness to mistakes means that the vast majority of your staff could be wrong. In order for you to move ahead and concurrently honor the minority view, a requirement of meaningful participation and shared responsibility is the assurance that the entire group will revisit the issue in the future. It even helps to set a certain time for revisiting the topic: six months, two years, or whatever seems reasonable to your staff, especially those who hold the minority perspective. Such assurance allows those who don't support the original consensus decision the opportunity to be heard again.

UNTANGLING COMPROMISE, CONSENSUS, AND UNANIMOUS CONSENT

Even if schools consistently apply the principles of consensus decision making, they sometimes drift from consensus to compromise. When your school staff compromises on an issue requiring meaningful participation and shared responsibility, you give up something you stand for in order to receive something in return. Operating under compromise conditions, problem solving may unfold in ways that don't match core values. Consider the following scenario:

It was four weeks from the end of the year at Briarcliff Elementary School and the staff was tired. They had implemented a new program for inclusion of special-needs children with little support outside the school and, though successful, the process had been exhausting.

Mr. Lecy, the teacher leader, just received word that a local foundation has awarded the school a $30,000 grant to establish a summer program for children with autism who attend Briarcliff. Because of Briarcliff's special-education program and commitment to inclusion for special-needs children, there were ten low-income children with autism in the school who have no summer program. Mr. Lecy knew this grant was bittersweet. On one hand, it offered the possibility of help for some of the children who needed it most and had little, or nothing, available. On the other hand, the teachers with the most knowledge and commitment to inclusion were the most exhausted among the staff. Just yesterday, Ms. Chilletti had told him how much she was looking forward to resting and replenishing during the summer. The deadline was short and implementation would have to begin in six weeks.

At the faculty meeting that afternoon, Mr. Lecy announced with excitement that the school had received a $30,000 award for the summer program and congratulated the grant writer, Ms. Chilletti. The staff stared back at him in disbelief. They knew it meant immediate and intense work to design a summer curriculum while conducting all the necessary scaling down, report writing, and cleaning that goes with the ending of the school year. They also knew how difficult the year had been for the staff involved in implementing the inclusion program.

Mrs. Revisio, the principal, immediately stepped in and said, "Okay, let's get started! What are the first steps we need to take to be ready for the summer program, Ms. Chilletti?" Ms. Chilletti immediately proposed turning the summer program over to Redwood, the local residential school. As rationale for her recommendation, she noted the short timeline and Redwood's expertise in summer programming. The staff ignored the fact that this meant the children who had been included with typical peers during the school year would spend the summer only with other children with autism, many of whom didn't speak. They readily agreed with Ms. Chilletti's suggestion and a decision was reached. They then moved on to the next agenda item.

Mr. Lecy was troubled and slept little that night. Early the next morning, he went to see Mrs. Revisio and explained his point of view:

> "We've committed ourselves to shared decision making, but yesterday's faculty meeting was more like "duck, duck, goose" with no one wanting to take responsibility for the grant. It goes against our value of inclusion and providing our children with autism with typical role models if we send them to Redwood. It was a compromise to avoid upsetting Ms. Chilletti."

Mrs. Revisio agreed with Mr. Lecy and asked him what thoughts he had about next steps.

On Friday, Mrs. Revisio announced that substitute teachers would be coming in on Monday afternoon to cover classes and that teachers should convene in the conference area at 12 noon. That afternoon, Mrs. Revisio went to see Ms. Chilletti. She began with honest appreciation for all Ms. Chilletti had accomplished in implementing the inclusion program. She talked about the strong match between the program and the core values of the school, that all children can learn. She acknowledged Ms. Chilletti's hard work and fatigue. She also asked, "What can we do about this summer program so that you have time to rest and recover from the school year and implement the program to support our value of including special needs children with typical children? Turning it over to Redwood is a compromise, but it is not consensus about what works best for our students." Ms. Chilletti agreed to think about it until Monday.

At Monday's faculty meeting, Ms. Revisio presented a similar position to the faculty. She began by honestly praising all that Ms. Chilletti had accomplished by including the special-needs children in her classroom. She also praised her for writing an award-winning grant. Mrs. Revisio went on to review the elements of the grant and to connect them with the values implemented throughout the school that year. She then asked the faculty the same question she'd posed to Ms. Chilletti: "How can we be sure that Ms. Chilletti gets the rest and recovery time she so richly deserves and find a way to implement the grant in a way that continues our loyalty to our core values?" By the end of the meeting, a plan was in place to release Ms. Chilletti two days a week until the end of school and to have her end-of-year responsibilities voluntarily assumed by other teachers. Additional accommodations were developed and the program was successfully implemented. Mr. Lecy and Mrs. Revisio were able to use "and" thinking to implement a program that was best for both the Briarcliff students and the Briarcliff teachers with no need for compromise.

Unlike compromise, consensus requires the flexibility to step away from defending positions and, instead, to move forward on what the school as a whole wants to accomplish and how the school wants to get there, together. Working within the framework of consensus, problem solving takes a different slant. At Briarcliff, Mrs. Revisio was able to involve the person with the most to gain and lose, Ms. Chilletti, in working with her and the staff to craft a solution. The resulting feeling about the summer program was so positive that it continued long after the grant expired. The students benefited; the staff benefited and became more skillful in knowing the difference between compromise and consensus.

To personalize the difference between the two concepts, compromise forces me to trade in something I value in order to get something I value a little more. Reciprocally, you do the same thing. We both compromise on what we value. In consensus building, we continue to work toward solving the problem with this touchstone: there is a solution yet to be discovered that allows each of us to maintain the integrity of our values and still find a mutually agreeable solution.

Consensus sometimes gets confused with unanimous agreement. Admittedly, the spirit of consensus suggests that your school should find a solution that everyone can happily support. In reality, you can expect occasions when repeated attempts to reach a workable solution end up with some individuals steadfastly opposing the "consensus" point of view. For instance, consider what the principal of a large elementary school in a border town told us:

> "I had a teacher come in the office after two hours of a team meeting, and she said she wasn't going to do what the group agreed to. So, I said, '"Then you have to figure out a way to get to the "'base'" at the same time the other teachers get to the "'base.'" So go home and think about it. And if you can't, you have two choices. You need to do what everybody else is doing, or you need to figure out

where you are working next year."' She came in the next day and said, "'I don't want to work anywhere else next year, and I can't figure out another way to get to the "'base'" at the same time, so here's the deal. I am going to do what everyone else is doing but I'm not happy about it."' And I said, "'That's fine. I can live with that. You are never going to have a perfect society.'"

In anticipation of circumstances like this, schools need to establish a ground rule within their consensus-building principles that addresses a last-resort measure. For example, your school could conclude that ultimately a group decision will be declared if at least 85 percent of the staff support the solution. The establishment of such a ground rule needs to be accompanied by two assurances. First, the 85 percent ground rule never will be applied until you have asked yourselves (collectively) key questions related to your core values. Referring to the Hague High School example, those questions could be:

- ♦ Have we *fully* involved everyone as participants in the problem-solving process?
- ♦ Have we listened *carefully* to all points of view, particularly the unpopular perspectives?
- ♦ Have we *seriously* faced any conflict emerging within our group and conscientiously tried to reconcile the differences?
- ♦ Have we *thoroughly* exhausted all possibilities for a quality decision, allowing ample time for reflection?
- ♦ Have we *openly* acknowledged that I could be wrong and you could be right, clearing the way for a solution that is stronger than any one perspective?

Out of respect for the professional judgment of the minority perspective, a second assurance needs to be granted: the group decision definitely will be revisited within a specified time period and the dissenting voices will again be listened to carefully. This provision minimizes the feeling of winners and losers. It also signals the flexibility of the group to reconsider decisions in the future.

In adopting a last-resort ground rule of defining consensus as a certain percentage of "yes" votes, your staff needs to make sure the ground rule is clearly a last resort. In other words, it does not become a shortcut for getting a quick resolution to move on to other things.

Are Consensus Decisions Binding?

The answer lies in understanding the distinction between shared governance and shared responsibility for decisions made. Shared governance assumes that all staff in the school have an equal voice in governing the school, resulting in equal accountability for actions. While this sharing of power has implicit appeal, in a practical sense schools need to come to grips with the level of accountability they want to assume. In other words, does a school (as a group) want to be held accountable for decisions such as dismissing a colleague teacher for misconduct? Does an entire school want to be held accountable for changing the schedule of the night custodian? Does a school council want to be held accountable when an irate employee complains to the school board that she was denied evening access to the school auditorium?

In the final analysis, most of the research on organizational effectiveness points to the organizational design where the school principal answers to his or her supervisor for the decisions made at the school level. In rare instances, therefore, we have found that, even in the spirit of shared responsibility for the direction of the school, the school principal can exercise "veto power" over the school's "consensus" decision. If the principal simply can't possibly defend the proposed consensus decision as being in the best interests of the school, then her or she should not be expected to defend it.

To better understand the implications of this apparent power, we need to clarify the phrase "rare instances." Running the risk of setting arbitrary standards, it seems reasonable to expect that at least 95 percent of the group decisions should be made *with* consensus and *without* veto. If a pattern of frequent vetoes occurs, the school principal and his or her supervisor need to start examining whether such practices are consistent with the values of the school in the areas of meaningful participation and shared responsibility and why the vetoes continue to occur.

Provide Training for Consensus-Building

One of the worst attempts at meaningful participation and shared responsibility occurs when school leaders turn staff loose to implement this value without the necessary training to be effective. Increased participation and responsibility with no training is sure to result in conflict among staff, the questioning of mutually agreed upon values, and frustration with the ideal of core values. Even if your school truly believes in the values, they may not have the skills to automatically make it happen. And why should we assume otherwise? Teachers are well educated about issues relating to curriculum and instruction and child development. Few have any experience in group processes with adults.

If teachers are cast into a group setting that calls for consensus decision making, yet they find themselves with nothing but the old rules to rely on, what can we expect to happen? The old rules evoke old behavior. So, inevitably, the individuals resort to power-and-control tactics because that's all they know how to use in group conflict situations. The end result is disaster. Staff members make themselves vulnerable by trusting the new values and then they get hurt because win-lose strategies emerge and the old value system kicks in. Consensus gives way to power plays and factions jockeying for their positions to prevail. People walk away mistrustful and blaming each other as well as the consensus process. In the future, these teachers return to the old way of doing business because at least they know how the game is played.

To avoid such disaster, don't avoid the training necessary to make consensus work. Many different consensus-training models are available to help groups work together effectively. There is no single recipe for success. There are, however, some basic training guidelines to look for in any program. The model discussed below illustrates how these guidelines have been successfully applied in several schools where we've worked. The model, taught to us by our colleague Bob Chadwick, requires very little equipment: a trained facilitator, enough chairs for everyone, no tables, enough easels with flipcharts and markers to accommodate group sizes of five to seven, and an appealing meeting environment.

Guideline 1: Honor the right of each colleague to speak without interruption, in an environment of trust and open communication. Most school leaders and staff have learned the hard way that groups frequently lack an environment of trust and open communication. In a consensus-building model, these important ingredients are developed as the facilitator moves the group through a series of steps. As an example, the facilitator can begin with a grounding activity that asks all group members to do the following:

- Introduce themselves.
- Describe their connection to the group.
- Comment on how they feel about being at the meeting.
- Describe their expectations for the meeting.

This simple grounding task is a powerful tool for setting the expectations that each person will be heard without interruption. How often do you remember beginning a meeting being able to comment in an environment that is respectful of each individual's statement, irrespective of his or her power status in the school? The grounding also establishes verbal territory for each participant, allowing his or her voice to be entered into the discussion early in the process. In turn, this initial commentary makes it easier for the individuals to speak later in the process.

Grounding also acknowledges that people have feelings that they bring to the group. It could be baggage from previous experience with the group; it could be strong emotions about the topic to be discussed; or it could be feelings about things that happened at home just prior to the meeting. Whatever the basis for emotions, feelings play a significant role in problem solving within an environment of trust and open communication. The grounding acknowledges the importance of feelings without pressing people to reveal intimate, personal thoughts that are best left private.

As a follow-up to the grounding activity, facilitators typically use both small-group and large-group activities to move people forward to resolution of the issues at hand. With each activity, school staffs develop greater assurance that they can speak and their remarks will be listened to with respect. The role of the facilitator is crucial to assure this safety, particularly with groups just embarking on the consensus-building process or those where there may be considerable tension.

Guideline 2: Move to the point of tension and begin problem solving in a non-threatening way. Generally the tendency of school staff is to avoid tension within group settings. People naturally want to mask the possible conflict and talk about more superficial issues. A role of the facilitator is to listen intently for the real issues of your group. If you use a facilitator who does not know the group or its history, the person will find it helpful to interview each participant prior to the session.

Once the real issues have been determined either inside or outside the session, the facilitator asks several people representing diverse perspectives to form a panel and speak to the issues, offering both what they think and how they feel about the issue. Although intelligent, educated professionals may argue that their decisions are based on logic, we've learned that all our decisions are a combination of thinking and feeling. Both reason and emotion are important considerations in arriving at collective decisions.

It is critical that the panel members are allowed to speak freely, without interruption or correction. At the completion of each person's statement, another panel member should be asked to repeat what was said. The facilitator guides the speaker and listener in an exchange that assures that the dialogue continues until the listener has repeated without bias or interpretation what the speaker said to the speaker's satisfaction. Then, and only then, the listener becomes the speaker and the process is repeated until all points of view are expressed and heard. A skillful facilitator may ask those most in opposition to "listen" to the opposing view and repeat for clarification.

As your staff begins to realize that they can speak safely on a given issue, they will begin to make themselves more vulnerable. It is also critical that, as a school leader, you participate in the process and make yourself vulnerable. Vulnerability allows you to be seen as an individual with identity, rather than just a position on the organizational chart. Also, as people become able to separate the issue from the personalities involved, they are more free to see tension as a positive energy leading you out of gridlock toward a solution all of you can support.

Guideline 3: Focus on best-case outcomes and press for creative solutions to achieve these outcomes. Typically schools find themselves stuck in a problem-solving process focusing on trying to keep the worst-case outcomes from happening. The more barriers you tear down, however, the more barriers you seem to discover. This approach to problem solving uses negative energy by pressing harder and harder against the restraining forces.

A training model for consensus decision making does not duck the worst-case outcomes. In fact, the model includes a step at the beginning of the process that asks the question, "What are the worst-case outcomes of not solving this problem?" By dealing with worst fears at the beginning, people are better able to answer the following questions: "What are the best-case outcomes of solving this problem? What are creative solutions for making the best-case outcomes happen?"

For virtually every school, the best solutions to the group's problems already exist within the expertise of the group. The facilitator is trained to connect various individuals' perspectives with "and" thinking, so that the collective wisdom is harnessed to reach rich collective decisions.

Guideline 4: Use a variety of problem-solving tools to move the group toward consensus. Some groups come together and just talk about the problem until they get too tired to do anything else but make a hurried decision so they can go home. Even though they have good intentions, they don't have a good stock of tools. The consensus model uses an array of problem-solving tools to help reach consensus. Depending on the size of the group and the nature of the issue, the facilitator can lead the group through activities such as nominal group process, fist-to-five consensus seeking, silent group sorting of ideas, determining priorities by spending tokens, and mapping cause and effect using branching diagrams. For more elaboration on these strategies, please refer to appendix B.

As stated earlier in this chapter, there are no shortcuts to achieving meaningful participation and shared responsibility for decisions. The strategies discussed above take time and perseverance, and above all the strategies demand an attention and commitment to the overall values held by the school. Is it worth the effort? Schools who have consistently applied the concepts outlined in this chapter swear they will never go back to the old top-down model of decision making. We think you will achieve similar results.

COLLECT FORMAL AND INFORMAL FEEDBACK ON LEADERSHIP TO CREATE MEANINGFUL PARTICIPATION AND SHARED RESPONSIBILITY

Throughout the book, we have repeatedly examined leadership strategies for school leaders who are committed to moving their schools ahead in spite of adversity. Also, we have repeatedly made the case that the administrators and teacher leaders are not solely responsible for achieving the seven strengths we have outlined. Indeed, school site councils, school staffs, and even the broader community have a responsibility to demonstrate these strengths. In particular, the feedback inventory form in fig. 8.1 is applicable for use by everyone responsible for moving the school

FIGURE 8.1 FEEDBACK INVENTORY ON MEANINGFUL PARTICIPATION AND SHARED RESPONSIBILITY

Instructions: For each key point, record your rating on a 1–5 scale. To indicate the level of *importance* you attribute to each key point, record the rating in the *Importance* column.

1	2	3	4	5
not important		somewhat important		highly important

To indicate the extent to which the key point has been *effectively implemented,* record the rating in the *Effectiveness* column.

1	2	3	4	5
not implemented		somewhat implemented		highly implemented

Compare the ratings to determine the *gap* between importance and effectiveness.

Key Point	Importance	Effectiveness	Gap
Achieve meaningful participation.			
Achieve shared responsibility for decisions.			
Develop processes for determining who decides how decisions get made.			
Develop consensus strategies based on core values.			
Encourage everyone to be a serious contributor.			
Acknowledge the presence of conflict and resolve it constructively.			
Be willing to make reasonable mistakes and admit it.			
Provide consensus-building training.			
Use a variety of problem-solving tools to move the group toward consensus.			

ahead. We strongly encourage school leaders to create expectations that individuals and groups will collect data relative to the extent that they value and effectively implement the key points about meaningful participation and shared responsibility.

We also encourage you, as a school leader, to gather informal data through the self-reflective questions below.

INFORMAL REFLECTION BY SCHOOL LEADERS

- ◆ What have I done to achieve meaningful participation by everyone affected by decisions?
- ◆ What have I done to achieve shared responsibility for decisions?
- ◆ To what extent have I developed processes for determining who decides how decisions get made?
- ◆ In what ways have I provided leadership to develop consensus strategies based on core values?
- ◆ To what extent have I encouraged everyone to be a serious contributor?
- ◆ In what ways have I acknowledged the presence of conflict and attempted to resolve it constructively?
- ◆ To what extent have I been willing to make reasonable mistakes and admit it?
- ◆ To what extent have I provided consensus-building training for staff?
- ◆ How have I used a variety of problem-solving tools to move the group toward consensus?

9

Putting It All Together!

The Collective Power of the Seven Strengths

Throughout this book we have built a strong foundation for helping schools move ahead in the face of adversity with seven strengths. In this chapter we turn our attention to the importance of harnessing all seven strengths together to move your school ahead. To set the stage, we begin with a case study of a school, facing an imposed change under conditions of adversity. Next we describe how the school applies the seven strengths in a resilient way. Finally, we show what happens to the dynamics when any one of the strengths is absent from the equation.

Two Rivers Community School's enrollment has been hovering around 2,000 students for the past ten years. Although their enrollment has been stable, other conditions have not. Two Rivers has experienced a decline in its economic base and a revolving-door pattern of school board membership.

However, Tony Ginelli, the principal, has been a steady force in guiding the school. He has consistently demonstrated solid leadership skills.

Today, however, Mr. Ginelli grapples with a new leadership challenge. Over the past seven years, Two Rivers Community School invested heavily in an instructional training model for teachers and administrators. Called the Quality Instruction Training (QIT) program, this model is based on the work of Research for Better Teaching. Applying the most current principles and best practices to improve student learning, QIT is designed to strengthen instructional skills for teachers and administrators. The training takes place over three years, with twenty-five hours per year devoted to skill building.

Two Rivers Community School revamped its teacher evaluation process to align with the QIT program. So the staff, administration, and even the community take pride in this home-grown initiative.

The leadership challenge is this: Yesterday the State Department of Education unveiled a mandatory teacher-training and evaluation program. This "Personnel Evaluation Plan" (PEP) is based on the following set of principles developed by a state task force:

◆ The primary goal of the evaluation program is the improvement of teaching and learning.

◆ A sound personnel evaluation program focuses on performance rather than credentials.

◆ A quality personnel evaluation program requires direct training of all staff affected by the program.

◆ Essential to any evaluation program is the identification of specific behaviors and practices that can be identified, assessed, and improved.

As Mr. Ginelli reviews the list, he realizes that the declared principles of the state program, PEP, align with the Two Rivers Community School model. However, PEP is not the Two Rivers model, and Mr. Ginelli's staff is proud of their program. As Mr. Ginelli rereads this latest state mandate, including the mandated elements of self-assessment, multiple observations, structured interviews of teachers, evaluation summary reports filed by each principal, and required action plans filed by each teacher, Mr. Ginelli wonders aloud, "How can we move ahead with our QIT initiative in the face of the latest state requirements on the same subject?"

As Mr. Ginelli ponders his own question, he grabs his well-worn copy of *Bouncing Back*. He quickly turns to the chapter on "Putting It All Together" to refresh his memory on the Seven Strengths of Resilient School Leaders. He uses the next three hours to sketch out a plan of action to apply the Seven Strengths to this new challenge. Specifically, he types notes to himself about strategies on how to move ahead with the school's commitment to QIT in the face of the state's sudden adoption of something called PEP. Here's what he typed under each strength:

STRENGTH #1: STAY FOCUSED ON CORE VALUES

My notes:

We have invested two long, hard years of our time and energy constructing core values about student learning. I remember with pride the feeling that permeated the room when our staff said "yes!" to the final draft of the following core value package we crafted:

We value putting improved student learning for all students at the center of everything we do. Therefore we will:

♦ Implement strategies for charting the progress of each student.
♦ Incorporate diverse teaching strategies that are responsive to the diverse learning styles of our students.
♦ Design teacher and administrator training around best practices.
♦ Avoid fads that take us away from these best practices.

I also remember my firm commitment to the staff that I will serve as a barrier to any new demands that don't square with these core values. I have tried to model this commitment on a regular basis and I can't let the state's newest idea called PEP take us off our game plan. Therefore, as we work through the anguish of responding to this state mandate, I will do whatever it takes to stay focused on our core values.

STRENGTH #2: MAINTAIN HIGH EXPECTATIONS FOR STUDENTS AND ADULTS

My notes:

In conjunction with our belief about improved student learning for *all* students, not just *some* of them, we have worked equally hard to keep our focus on high expectations for all students, no matter what excuses may tempt us to lower our standards. Using our benchmarks from QIT, we aligned our curriculum and instructional practices consistent with QIT. We also held our staff accountable for teaching to achieve these benchmarks. Our personnel evaluation process is integrally tied to these expectations. I'm sure the staff remembers when we had to dismiss a teacher who refused to "buy in" to the standards we set for acceptable teaching performance.

As we confront this new state mandate, some staff may see this as a way of relieving some of the pressures QIT puts on them. However, most of the staff will not want to give up what we have worked for. My job is to keep us on track about high expectations for students and staff despite this PEP stuff. I will not let us be deterred from the expectations we set. And I will continue to search the PEP model for any ways that we can link our own high expectations.

Strength #3: Create a Climate of Caring and Support

My notes:

Even though adversity has hit our school budget, I worked extremely hard to show that I care about people's financial concerns. I have made myself readily available to listen to any staff member talk about how the budget squeeze affects him or her. In the face of tough times, I have tried to reorder budget priorities to make sure that the focus of our spending is on student learning, above all else. Now that we have this new challenge, the state-imposed program of teacher evaluation tied to imposed teaching standards, Two Rivers School will need to protect what we have built around the value of caring and support. A top-down initiative like PEP can get translated by teachers as "we don't care what you think out there in the schools."

But I will not let people get down on themselves. We have complete control of how we choose to react to imposed changes. We're not going let outsiders' actions affect our caring environment. I will continue to provide support in other ways. Granted, the budget is tight. At the same time, I can find support in the form of released time for teachers even if it means we bend the rules and bring in parents to cover classes for part of a day. And I will continue to volunteer to substitute-teach in classes, as needed, if teachers have to go to mandated PEP training.

STRENGTH #4: TAKE CHARGE!

My notes:

I can tell very clearly that, as tired as our staff feels right now, this latest state mandate may push some very dedicated staff members over the edge from guarded optimist to flagrant pessimist. It sure doesn't look like this issue is going to disappear. So I need to take immediate action before a pessimistic cloud settles over the school.

The worst-case outcomes of ignoring this issue will be people giving up on our own program. However, the best-case outcomes of taking swift action to find a win-win solution between QIT and PEP will be continued support of QIT. The staff knows that I am strong in my convictions that our program is good for students and staff. I can't let them down, even if it means bending the rules of PEP to maintain the integrity of QIT. So I am willing to take risks to map out a plan of action that shows our staff how we can move ahead on what we believe and, at the same time, comply with the state mandate.

STRENGTH #5: REMAIN FLEXIBLE IN HOW YOU GET THERE

My notes:

If I look back on the principles of PEP that were published by the State Department of Education, many of the points sound somewhat similar to our own core values. The implementation of the points is another matter. When our staff reads the thick manual of imposed "rules," they are going to initially feel like all of their hard work has been flushed down the drain. I need to realize that they need time to vent and complain, so I have to be careful that I don't try to squelch their expression of feelings. I also have to be careful not to let them wallow too long in self-pity. In another words, there is a fine line between natural grieving and prolonged mourning as victim. I need to recognize the line so we don't cross it.

Plus, I need to remember that the State Department of Education is not clear yet on how it is going to handle districts who can demonstrate that they have solid practices already in place that conform to the PEP guiding principles. In other words, the state is going to be in Tweener Time for about a year. If we move swiftly to get a set of recommendations to the state, showing them how we can fulfill the expectations being laid on us within a framework that enjoys widespread support within the school, maybe our creative approach will be a model for how the state deals with other districts who also have sound programs in this area.

And circumstances may dictate that we have to be flexible in how we approach our own training and evaluation practices. If we have to give up some of the details of our own plan to conform to the state's mandates, it may be a small price to pay—as long as we can be true to our own core values. So I need to work within the imposed constraints of the state and still show that we can accomplish what we believe in at the school level. And who knows? The perspective of the creators of the PEP program may reveal some insights we haven't considered. I need to make sure we are open to hearing perspectives different from our own.

STRENGTH #6: BE POSITIVE IN SPITE OF ADVERSITY

My notes:

I have been in this business long enough to know that things don't always go the way we like. As it said in *Bouncing Back*, once a decision has been made at a higher level, I need to show the kind of leadership that helps our staff see the possibilities, not just the obstacles. The staff will be watching me very, very closely to see how I react to the PEP mandate. If I model a resilient response, it will help reassure them that this latest so-called surprise from the State Department of Education isn't all that big a deal. We will find ways to think "how can we" make it work, rather than dwell on the negative, "we can't make it work."

And I need to remember that humor has carried us through a lot of adversity. I can remind the staff that this latest move is predictable based on a pattern of other crazy ideas that have been handed down. They'll get a chuckle out of that. Besides, when I was telling them last week about how surprised I was that the school board made a certain decision on graduation requirements, they were quick to say, "Don't you remember what you taught us, Mr. Ginelli? You taught us not to spend resilience points on being surprised. It only counts when you are surprised you are surprised."

I can hear the staff laughingly saying the same thing about PEP: "We aren't surprised we're surprised." I need to use this kind of humor to keep us focused on the positive.

STRENGTH #7: CREATE MEANINGFUL PARTICIPATION AND SHARED RESPONSIBILITY

My notes:

My natural "Type A" personality is to grab hold of this monster called PEP and tame it. I know that some of the staff would stand on the sideline and cheer me on as I do battle with PEP. I also know from lapsing into this leadership style in the past that the short-term effect feels good, but the long-term impact is a lack of staff ownership.

When it comes to this most recent imposed change, I need to draw on our consensus-building model that has served us so well in the past. First of all, we need to be clear on "who decided who decides?" In this situation, I believe the staff needs to decide "who decides." I'm rather confident that they will want to use the guidelines we have adopted for consensus as ground rules for deciding how to move ahead on this issue. I need to keep us focused on the ground rules, play an active role in the process, and not push for a particular solution that happens to be my number one choice. In the end, the collective wisdom in the group will yield a richer solution than whatever solution I personally may fall in love with.

The above scenario illustrates the dynamics of how the Seven Strengths of Resilient School Leaders can create a powerfully resilient approach to resolving the QIT-PEP struggle at Two Rivers

Community School. Collectively the Seven Strengths form a strong foundation for moving ahead in the face of adversity. Notice what happens, however, when you as a school leader leave out any single strength from the total equation.

Without the leadership strength of *staying focused,* you have no center. In other words, if as a school leader you respond to PEP (or any other imposed change) without a clear, comprehensive picture of what you and the school stand for relative to the topic, you end up responding in the typical event-driven pattern. You react to the advent of PEP with criticism of the imposed change, letting people know you don't stand for PEP. But, without focus, you don't have anything to offer regarding what you *do* stand for. You waste resilience points flailing against the bureaucracy, when you could be conserving resilience points if you knew what you wanted to advocate in the place of PEP. Over time, a school without focus will find that the cumulative impact of constantly complaining about "what others are doing to us" will be manifest in a dried-up resilience account.

Without the leadership strength of *maintaining high expectations,* the natural tendency is to drift toward lowering the bar when the going gets tough. Even during so-called normal times, school staff exert a lot of energy and consume resilience points trying to meet the demands of high expectations. Adverse conditions consume more energy and more resilience. Lowering expectations can temporarily lower the pressure point. In the case of the issues surrounding PEP, it is tempting for school leaders to reduce the pressure, at least for the moment, by not holding staff accountable for trying to find creative solutions to accommodate both PEP and QIT principles. When the school leader abandons the rigor of high expectations for moving ahead, a climate gets established that responds to imposed change by saying, "Whatever they make us do, we'll comply." With such a mindset, the school leaders and school staff succumb to the drift toward mediocrity.

Without the leadership strength of *creating a climate of caring and support,* school leaders plow ahead with the agenda, irrespective of the emotional needs of the staff. In the above scenario, Mr. Ginelli could move ahead with whatever is decided about PEP, without consulting the staff regarding what they feel and what they are concerned about. Some school leaders respond to imposed change by conveying the attitude "Here's what is being mandated, here's what we need to do as a school to comply, and we have no choice except do it! So we need to get a grip on things, act like grown-ups and implement what is expected." So it is indeed possible to fulfill the leadership challenge of implementing PEP, even in connection with QIT, and do so in a way that produces an uncaring, unsupportive school environment.

Without the leadership strength of *taking charge*, schools play the waiting game to see what is going to happen to them. When an imposed change like PEP reaches the schools, many schools don't reach out to understand what is expected and what is possible. Instead, the school leader counsels the staff to withhold action, hoping by some miracle that PEP will vaporize. If Two Rivers Community School just waits and watches, likely there will be no short-term negative effects. The long-term effect, however, of Mr. Ginelli's not taking charge of the situation is a loss of control by the school over its own destiny. By not taking charge, Two Rivers by default places the state in charge of what happens to them. The fallout includes also placing blame on the state for what happens to them.

Without the leadership strength of *remaining flexible* in how you get to where you want to be, you limit both the range and quality of your options. Applied to the PEP mandate, Mr. Ginelli could legitimately argue that Two Rivers has set in motion a set of strategies to move them effectively and efficiently toward their goal. With a sense of pride and ownership, the school could justify with solid data how their path is the preferred one. However, when adversity arrives at Two Rivers in the form of imposed change, imagine what happens when Mr. Ginelli and staff force a showdown with the state by arguing "it's our way or the state's way. There is no other way. We don't intend to cave in to the pressures of the state." In such situations, schools usually come out on the losing side, because they have drawn a definite line in the sand and dared the other side to cross over it. In the end, an unwillingness to be flexible in how you achieve what is important will likely result in your not achieving it.

Without the leadership strength of *being positive* in the face of adversity, the entire school can quickly become enveloped in a shroud of gloom. Both Mr. Ginelli and his fellow principal at a nearby school can demonstrate the other six leadership strengths relative to PEP. However, the overall impact on the two schools will be qualitatively different if Mr. Ginelli takes the stance that the "glass is half empty" while his colleague views the glass as half full. More pointedly, imagine that Mr. Ginelli concludes his remarks to staff about PEP by saying, "I don't know why the state keeps picking on us. They won't let us do what we want to do. Everything we have worked for in our QIT has been rendered useless. Who knows what they will do to us next?" With this negative attitude by the leadership, you can also imagine the resilience drain on the staff. Growing out of such a negative tone is a growing hopelessness about achieving anything positive from the imposed mandate.

Without the leadership strength of *creating meaningful participation and shared responsibility*, the school leader assumes all of the burden of making things happen. If Mr. Ginelli announced to his staff, "Here's the situation and here's what we are going to do about it," the staff likely will feel short-term relief that they don't have to worry about the conflicts between PEP and QIT. In the longer run, however, school leaders need the support, the energy, and also the philosophical buy-in by staff to muster what it takes to move ahead in the face of adversity. Too many leaders have been seduced by the overt signals by the staff who say, "Go for it, boss. We're right behind you." Then, a few months later, when the boss turns around to reach for his or her support base, the realization sets in that the staff isn't "right behind you." They are so far behind you they can't be seen. Without a climate of meaningful participation and shared responsibility, the staff can legitimately say, "It was the leader's idea. We weren't involved in shaping our direction or our strategy, so we understandably aren't invested in it."

As we have learned from our research and shared with you throughout this book, each of the seven leadership strengths is critical for helping your school move ahead in the face of adversity. We want to underscore, one more time, that these strengths aren't reserved exclusively for the so-called formal leaders of the organization. Indeed, these strengths were exemplified just as prominently by the informal teacher leaders of schools. So whatever your formal title or your informal role in your organization, each of the strengths will take you and your school a long way to moving ahead during the tough times.

Collectively, these seven leadership strengths will help move your organization ahead to places you never imagined. Enjoy your journey!

Appendix A

Research Base for the Seven Strengths of Resilient School Leaders

RESEARCH ON RESILIENT SCHOOLS

Nan Henderson and Mike Milstein (1996) developed a model of a resilient school that includes characteristics of the environment for adults and students. Milstein and Doris Annie Henry (1999) broadened the conceptual framework even more to include schools and the community. The original model, called the Resiliency Wheel, is described fully in Henderson and Milstein's work (1996), and shown in fig. A.1 to provide you with a picture that includes most of the recognized theory on what a resilient school looks like.

'In this book we consider the deeper impact of three of the six factors from Henderson and Milstein's work on the schools. Based on our conversations with school leaders in the schools we visited, caring relationships, positive, high expectations, and meaningful participation are critical to resilience.

CARING RELATIONSHIPS

Teachers demonstrate their love, support, and belief in children by treating them kindly, and with compassion and respect. They listen to students and validate their feelings without judgment or taking the student's behavior as a personal affront.

School leaders intent on building resilient schools demonstrate their commitment to creating a caring environment through attitudes and behaviors. For instance, they will know names of students and staff, they will encourage the use of time to connect students and staff in "buddy" or mentoring programs, and they may even create formal recognitions for random acts of kindness. Caring will become institutionalized, woven into the cultural

FIGURE A.1 PROFILE OF A RESILIENCE-BUILDING SCHOOL

- Student viewed as workers and teachers as coaches.
- Everybody's contributions viewed as important.
- Members grow and learn by sharing, treating each other with respect.
- Experimentation is encouraged.

- Positive and supportive organizational climate and culture exists.
- Equity, risk taking, and learning are promoted.
- Visions and missions are clean, communicated, and agreed upon.

- Indiual efforts viewed as important.
- Risk taking promoted.
- "Can do!" attitudes prevail.
- Individualized growth plans developed and monitored

- Cooperation and support exist.
- Schoolwide objectives are shared.
- Members are involved in setting policies and rules.

Build Resiliency in the Environment

Mitigate Risk Factors in the Environment

Provide Opportunities for Meaningful Participation

Increase Prosocial Bonding

Set and Communicate High Expectations

Set Clear, Consistent Boundaries

Provide Caring & Support

Teach "Life Skills"

- Members have sense of belonging.
- Cooperation is promoted.
- Celebrations of successes are practiced.
- Leaders spend lots of positive time with members.
- Resources are obtained with a minimum of efforts.

- Efforts are made to improve the school.
- Risk taking is supported, as are individual and group skill development.
- Positive role modeling is practiced.

Source: Henderson, N. & Milstein, M (1996). *Resiliency in Schools,* Thousand Oaks, CA: Corwin Press.

fabric of the school. The "goodies" available in the school, the resources of time and money, will be shared among activities that promote caring and the belief that all can succeed.

POSITIVE, HIGH EXPECTATIONS

It is well established that teachers' expectations become self-fulfilling prophecies. Positive, high expectations convey to students that teachers believe in their ability to succeed. Expectations can guide student behavior and even lead students beyond what they believed possible. Positive, high expectations are particularly important for those students who may face the greatest adversity as they shift self-perception from victim to survivor (Wolin and Wolin, 1993).

In a similar fashion, school leaders committed to building resilient schools focus on leadership strategies that communicate positive, high expectations that everyone, students and staff, can succeed. Responsibility for teaching and learning is placed where it belongs: with teachers to teach effectively and students to learn. Specific strategies might include frequent assessment for students and teachers to measure success, opportunities to give and receive help, and celebrating successes schoolwide. Active involvement, accountability. and responsible decision making are key to optimizing high expectations.

MEANINGFUL PARTICIPATION

Resilience-building teachers believe in students expressing their opinions, using their talents, making choices, and working with and helping others. These teachers provide a physically and psychologically safe place for meaningful participation to occur and heartily encourage students to get involved in their schools and communities (Rutter et al., 1979; Rutter, 1984).

For school leaders, providing ways for students and staff to become meaningfully involved in the school is a high priority in building resilience. Leaders develop strategies that encourage cooperation and include all constituents in the school community, including the so-called "nay sayers", in issues relating to the school program. They find ways to communicate that "you are doing important work." Full participation and accompanying recognition of everyone in the school community is necessary to build a resilient environment.

Growing out of the research on resilient students, a number of educational programs and reforms were initiated in the last two decades. Many of them created conditions that result in positive outcomes for students, such as positive social behaviors, healthy physical development, increased student learning, and positive self-concepts. Examples of programs designed to strengthen students' skills with the goal of making them more resilient include:

- ◆ Accelerated Schools
- ◆ Adaptive Learning Environments Model
- ◆ Coalition of Essential Schools
- ◆ Higher Order Thinking Skills (HOTS)
- ◆ School Development Program
- ◆ Success for All

Even though many of these programs have been successful in improving student learning in specific areas, the insidious issues wrought by adversity cannot be solved solely by "canned programs." Systemic change to strengthen school resilience can only come about through the strength of resilient leadership.

THE RESEARCH BASE ON LEADERSHIP RESILIENCE

Historically, organizational resilience has been associated with dynamic leaders who thrive on performing under pressure. One of the earliest research studies (Kobasa, 1979) on leadership resilience identified the traits of resilience as activeness, self-reliance, and zest for living. More recently, Daryl Conner, in *Managing at the Speed of Change* (1992), found that resilient business leaders demonstrate certain characteristics that we have found also hold true for education leaders.

POSITIVE

Positive leaders display a sense of security and self-assurance that is based on their view of life as complex but filled with opportunities. Positive leaders also expect life to be filled with disruptions. In other words, they know that there will be adversity, or bumps along the road. And even though they don't know the exact formation of the bumps, leaders who are positive aren't surprised by the bumps. Indeed, the leaders believe that there are certain lessons to be learned from the bumps, twists, and turns along the journey.

FOCUSED

Focused leaders have a clear sense of what they want to achieve, even in the face of adversity. This is manifest in leaders maintaining and acting on a strong sense of purpose and values. Focused leaders can be spotted continuously orienting their organization to the values that are guiding them to the future. In fact, focused leaders maintain a perspective for the long haul. Rather than operating with a ninety-day planning horizon, these leaders are relentlessly asking the question "Where do we want to be three years from now?"

FLEXIBLE

Flexible leaders have a high tolerance for ambiguity. This is particularly critical during adverse times. Resilient leaders are tolerant of new, unfamiliar situations and are willing to act on incomplete, sometimes seemingly contradictory information. They also bounce back quickly from setbacks and seek alternative paths to achieve what matters most. Finally, flexible leaders seek to accommodate diverse perspectives. They pay attention to the messages sent by dissident voices and search for ways to incorporate diverse perspectives without giving up on their ultimate focus.

PROACTIVE

Adversity can bring out the competitive spirit in leaders. For resilient leaders, one key to being effective is knowing how to respond to adversity. In the face of adversity, resilient leaders aren't afraid to let go of the old way of doing things. They realize that blind adherence to the old ways can be detrimental to their resilience account. Proactive leaders also take risks in spite of potentially adverse consequences. If their actions are consistent with what they value, the long-term payoff for them and the organization is a greater sense of confidence that resilience points are being spent in a manner that aligns actions and values, irrespective of the consequences.

Conner's work combines with the work of Henderson and Milstein to provide a solid, research-based foundation for our Seven Strengths of Resilient Leaders.

THE SPECIAL CASE FOR TEACHER LEADERS AND RESILIENCE

Even though the characteristics outlined above were built from research on leaders in top leadership roles, we have learned through our work on resilience that the idea of resilient leaders does not reside exclusively with those sitting in the administrator's chair. Granted, twenty years ago writers argued that if the principal directed the work of teachers, held high expectations, and aligned the curriculum, then teachers would work cooperatively, schools would be effective, and principals would be considered strong leaders.

But experience and recent research have shed more light on the topic. In the old days of school hierarchies, the emphasis was on specialization, delegation, and efficiency. In today's world of shared decision making, the emphasis is on collaboration, consensus on goals, and shared responsibilities. Today, the evidence is clear that teacher leaders within schools contribute a great deal to strengthening school resilience.

When we talk about teacher leadership, we mean the *ability to support and encourage other teachers to do things they might not have considered without leadership from a trusted colleague* (Wasley, 1991). Teachers amplify the importance of teacher leaders when they say that the best way to influence their professional practice is to provide time for them to learn from and work with colleagues. Common sense and available data convince us that collegial interactions are key to building the collaborative culture associated with school resilience (Rosenholtz, 1991).

Teachers operating as leaders occupy various roles, including head teachers, department chairs, mentor teachers, team leaders, grade-level chairs, staff development trainers, and curriculum developers. Others, teacher leaders without such titles, sometimes offer workshops to their peers and act as a "critical friend" to support other teachers' professional growth.

Ann Lieberman, a renowned scholar on teacher behavior, articulated our perspective on the role of teacher leaders in creating a resilient school when she said, "Teacher participation in leadership may be the most critical component of the entire process of change" (Lieberman, 1992).

In the changing field of research on resilience, we have witnessed in the past twenty years three major paradigm shifts in thinking. First there has been a shift away from the deficits model that places an emphasis on fixing the areas where students and schools are broken. The shift has been towards a value-added model that emphasizes strengthening the areas where students and schools can grow the most. Currently, in the area of resilient leadership, researchers are asking "What are the strengths among resilient leaders that contribute to resilience?"

A second paradigm shift is movement away from an emphasis on programs and toward an emphasis on processes. In the past, researchers looked for effective programs or packages to install that would produce resilience; often, however, the programs vaporized when the funding that supported them disappeared. Here we move toward creating a resilient culture based on what you care about and processes that support the culture in an enduring way.

A third paradigm shift occurred with the recognition of the critical role played by teacher leaders in creating cultures that foster school resilience. Indeed, we found throughout our own research that teacher leaders were instrumental in moving the school ahead.

Appendix B

Tools for Reaching Group Consensus

1. Nominal Group Process

Purpose: To gather and rank various solutions to a problem.

Time Needed: Approximately 45 minutes.

Procedure:

1. Begin with a clear written statement of the problems to be addressed.
2. Ask each person to spend about 10 minutes writing ideas and responses on cards or a worksheet.
3. Form groups of ten or fewer and have everyone report out, round robin, each person giving one idea. Write each idea on a chart. Continue taking turns until all ideas are on the chart. Ideas may be clarified as you go, or clarified when all ideas are charted. Clarification is aimed at making the ideas understandable, not editing or eliminating them.
4. Ask participants in the group to list on cards the best four, five, or six ideas (whatever number seems to produce a suitable range). These ideas are then listed on a separate chart.
5. These may be further ranked by having each person assign each idea a rating of 1 to 5. Total rankings for each item to determine highest priorities.

2. Fist to Five

Purpose: To poll the group's feelings at any point in a discussion.

Time Needed: Approximately 3 to 5 minutes.

Procedure:
    When asked to show a fist to five, participants show:

    ♦ Fist: absolutely not, or disagree.
    ♦ Three fingers: neutral.
    ♦ Five fingers: total agreement.

3. BRAINSTORMING

Purpose: To generate numerous ideas in a short period of time.

Time Needed: Approximately 15 minutes.

Rules for Brainstorming:

    ♦ No criticism allowed.
    ♦ No explanations needed.
    ♦ Be freewheeling; anything goes.
    ♦ Seek combinations and improvements.
    ♦ Seek quantity over quality.
    ♦ Be spontaneous; don't respond in any predetermined
      order.

4. SORTING

Purpose: To distill brainstormed lists to a workable number of ideas.

Time Needed: Approximately 10 minutes.

Procedure:

    1. After brainstorming ways to accomplish a specific
       goal, post three large sheets of chart paper.
    2. Ask the group to sort the ideas into three categories:
       ♦ Quick fixes: Those ideas that are important and can
         be accomplished quickly or by one individual.
       ♦ Out of our hands: Ideas that are not realistic given
         our present circumstances.
       ♦ Definite possibilities: The rest of the ideas.
    3. Concentrate future team efforts on the Definite
       Possibilities list. Eliminate the Out of Our Hands list,
       but don't ignore the ideas in the Quick Fix list, for they
       may be the source of early and easy successes.
       Individual volunteers may tackle those issues, freeing
       the group to address more complex ideas.

5. CLUSTERING

Purpose: Use to merge small-group ideas into a total group product.

Time Needed: Approximately 40 minutes.

Procedure:

1. Ask small groups to brainstorm the solution to a problem or to generate goals on slips of paper (8 1/2" x 11" paper cut lengthwise works nicely, as do large Post-it notes). Each brainstormed idea should be written on a separate slip.
2. After the small groups have completed brainstorming, ask one group to post one of their ideas on the wall. Ask other groups if they have any similar ideas and tape those slips directly beneath the first.
3. Ask a second group to post another idea on the wall and again ask other groups to put similar ideas beneath this one. Continue categorizing the slips in this manner until all ideas are posted.
4. Review the columns of ideas with the group and then ask them to label each of the categories. (The label should capture the essence of each cluster.) Proceed with some type of ranking procedure, such as a variation of the Nominal Group Process or Spend a Buck.

6. SPEND A BUCK

Purpose: To provide a ranking system.

Time Needed: Approximately 15 minutes.

Procedure:

1. Distribute 3" x 5" cards to participants and ask them to write each predetermined issue or category on a card. Each participant will need as many cards as there are issues.
2. When they have finished, inform them that they have one dollar to spend. The task is to determine which idea or ideas are most important and then divide their money accordingly. Participants write on each card how much they are willing to spend on that item.

3. Remind participants that no one can spend more than a dollar.
4. Collect the cards and tabulate.

7. THE 1-3-6 TECHNIQUE

Purpose: To obtain information when group members are reluctant to speak or when some group members tend to dominate. This is an easy and fair way to prioritize issues in a relatively short time.

Time Needed: Approximately 35 minutes.

Procedure:

1. State the topic and allow two to three minutes for each person to list one or two ideas concerning the topic on a card.
2. Form the participants into groups of three (either voluntary or assigned groups). The groups of three discuss the ideas of each person in the group and select one or two ideas that the group can support. This usually takes 7 to 10 minutes.
3. Once each group has selected its priorities, its members should join another group to form a group of six. Again, the goal is to discuss the choices and choose the best one or two items to represent this group of six.
4. Ideas from the groups of six are charted for everyone to see. Every person is given five sticker dots and must choose what he or she believes are the best alternatives. All five dots cannot be put on one alternative; they must be divided in some way among the alternatives. The results are graphic and apparent to all.

8. THE FISHBOWL

Purpose: To discuss the ideas generated in small groups in a large-group setting.

Time Needed: Depends on topic; usually 30 to 60 minutes.

Procedure:

1. Form a circle of chairs in the middle of the room (one chair per group plus one additional chair).

2. Brainstorm responses and record all ideas on Post-it notes or cards, follow hints for brainstorming.
3. Randomly place the Post-it notes or cards on chart paper, a blackboard, a tabletop, or another flat surface.
4. Push for breakthrough thinking, then end verbal brainstorming.
5. Ask participants to silently sort random ideas into categories by placing like ideas in the same area.
6. Participants continue moving and removing Post-it notes or cards.
7. Consensus is reached when no one moves any more Post-it notes or cards.
8. Ask participants to develop a category statement that describes the essence of the ideas in each category, and place this statement at the top of each category, as shown in the diagram below.
9. Ask participants to prioritize categories using common sense or other prioritization tools.
10. See below for an example of the product from a silent consensus.

9. Tree Diagram

Purpose: To help move goals to implementation

Time Needed: 1 to 1 1/2 hours

Procedure:

1. Place a goal statement to the extreme left center of a piece of chart paper.
2. Ask the group, "What target objectives do we need to meet to accomplish this goal?"
3. Write answers to this question on Post-it notes placed to the right of the goal statement (see below).
4. Ask the following question of each target objective: "What activities, projects, processes need to be accomplished to achieve this target objective?"
5. Write answers to this question of Post-it notes placed to the right of each target objective (see diagram).
6. Assign each of the activities, projects, and processes generated to a person who will assume responsibility for completing the task.
7. Timelines for completion can also be added.

RESULTS OF SILENT CONSENSUS

Category

Category

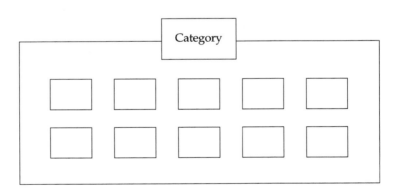

Category

TREE DIAGRAM

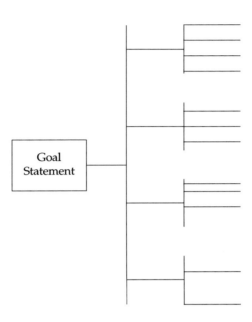

Recommended Readings

STUDENTS

Benard, B. (1995). *Fostering resilience. ERIC Digest.* Urbana, Ill.: ERIC.

Benard, B. (1992). *Fostering resiliency in kids: Protective factors in the family, school, and community.* Portland, Ore.: Western Regional Center for Drug-Free Schools and Communities, Northwest Educational Laboratory.

Garmezy, N. (1985). Stress resilient children: The search for protective factors. In J. E. Stevenson (Ed.), *Recent research in developmental psychopathology: Journal of Child Psychology and Psychiatry book.* (Supplement 4). Oxford: Pergamon Press.

Grotberg, E. H. (1996). The international resilience project: Research and application. In E. Miao (Ed.), *Proceedings of the 53rd annual convention of the International Council of Psychologists. Cross-cultural encounters.* Taipei, Taiwan: General Innovation Service.

Grotberg, E. H. (1997). The international resilience project. In B. Bain (Ed.), *Proceedings of the 54th annual convention of the International Council of Psychologists.* Edmonton, Canada: ICP Press.

Patterson, J. H. (2001). Raising resilience in classrooms and homes. *Childhood Education* (Spring).

Werner, E., and R. Smith (1992). *Overcoming the odds: High risk children from birth to adulthood.* Ithaca, NY: Cornell University Press.

Werner, E., and R. Smith (1982). Vulnerable but invincible: A study of resilient children. New York: McGraw-Hill.

Wolin, S. J., and S. Wolin (1994). *Survivor's pride: Building resilience in youth at risk* (video). Verona, Wis.: Attainment Company.

LEADERS

Bridges, W. (1991). *Managing transition: Making the most of change.* Reading, Mass.: Addison-Wesley.

Brandt, R. (1989). On teacher empowerment: A conversation with

Ann Lieberman. *Educational Leadership* 46, 23–26.

Cawelti, G. (1989). Key elements of site-based management. *Educational Leadership* 46, 46.

Conner, D. R. (1992). *Managing at the speed of change.* New York: Random House.

Conner, D. R. (1996). The structure of change. *Executive Excellence* 13 (3), 6.

Conner, D. R. (1998). *Leading at the edge of chaos.* New York: John Wiley & Sons.

Doe, P. J. (1994). Creating a resilient organization. *Canadian Business Review* (summer), 22–25.

Fessler, R., and A. Ungaretti (1994). Expanding opportunities for teacher leadership. In D. R. Walling (Ed.), *Teachers as leaders: Perspective on the professional development of teachers.* Bloomington, Ind.: Phi Delta Kappa Educational Foundation.

Grotberg, E. H. (1999). *Tapping your inner strength.* Oakland, Calif.: New Harbinger Publications.

Lieberman, A.; Saxl, E. R., and M. B. Miles (1988). Teacher leadership: Ideology and practice. In A. Lieberman (Ed.), *Building a professional culture in schools,* 148–166. New York: Teachers College Press.

Little, J. W. (1988). Assessing the prospects for teacher leadership. In A. Lieberman (Ed.), *Building a professional culture in schools,* 78–106. New York: Teachers College Press.

Little, J. W. (1990). The persistence of privacy: Autonomy and initiative in teachers' professional relations. *Teachers College Record* 91: 509–536.

Maddi, S. (1984). *The hardy executive: Health under stress.* Homewood, Ill.: Dow Jones-Irwin.

Moller, G. (1999). You have to want this job. *Journal of Staff Development* 20, 4, 10–16.

Patterson, J. L. (1993). *Leadership for tomorrow's schools.* Alexandria, Va.: Association for Supervision and Curriculum Development.

Patterson, J. L. (1997). *Coming clean about organizational change.* Arlington, Va.: American Association of School Administrators.

Patterson, J. L. (2000). *The anguish of leadership.* Arlington, Va.: American Association of School Administrators.

Patterson, J. (2001). Resilience in the face of adversity. *The School Administrator* 58, 6, 18–24.

Patterson, J. L., and J. H. Patterson (2001). Resilience in the face of imposed changes. *Principal Leadership* 1, 6, 50–55.

Rosenholtz, S. J. (1991). *Teacher's workplace: The social organization of schools*. New York: Teachers College Press.

Wasley, P. A. (1991). *Teachers who lead: The rhetoric of reform and the realities of practice*. New York: Teachers College Press.

Wasley, P. A. (1994). *Stirring the chalkdust: Tales of teachers changing classroom practice*. New York: Teachers College Press.

Watkins-Johnson. (1996). Building workforce resilience: A guide to launching a process. U.S. Economic Development Administration, Joint Venture: Silicon Valley Network Resources.

Weick, K. (1996). Prepare your organization to fight fires. *Harvard Business Review* (May–June), 143–148.

SCHOOLS

Anderson, G., K. Herr, and A. Nihlen (1994). *Studying your own school*. Thousand Oaks, Calif.: Corwin Press.

Anderson, L. (1994). Effectiveness and efficiency in inner-city public schools: Charting school resilience. In M. C. Wang and E. W. Gordon (Eds.), *Educational resilience in inner-city America: Challenges and prospects*, 141–150. Hillsdale, N.J.: Lawrence Erlbaum.

Bacharach, S. B. (1986). The learning workplace: The conditions and resources of teaching. Washington, D.C.: National Education Association.

Comer, J. P. (1980). *School power*. New York: The Free Press.

Freiberg, J. H. (1994). Understanding resilience: Implications for inner-city schools and their near and far communities. In M. C. Wang and E. W. Gordon (Eds.), *Educational resilience in inner-city America: Challenges and prospects*, 151–166. Hillsdale, N.J.: Lawrence Erlbaum.

Henderson, N., and M. Milstein (1996). *Resiliency in schools: Making it happen for students and educators*. Thousand Oaks, Calif.: Corwin Press.

Krovetz, M. (1999). *Fostering resiliency: Expecting all students to use their minds and hearts well*. Thousand Oaks, Calif.: Corwin Press.

Milstein, M., and D. A. Henry (1999). *Spreading resiliency: Making it happen for schools and community*. Thousand Oaks, Calif.: Corwin Press.

Wang, M. C., and E. W. Gordon (Eds.) (1994). *Educational resilience in inner city America: Challenges and Prospects*. Hillsdale, N.J.: Lawrence Erlbaum.

References

Benard, B. (1991). *Fostering resiliency in kids: Protective factors in the family, school, and community*. Portland, OR: Northwest Regional Educational Laboratory.

Bridges, W. (1991). *Managing transitions: Making the most of change*. Reading, Mass.: Addison-Wesley.

Bridges, W. (2001). *The way of transition: Embracing life's most difficult moments*. Perseus Books.

Conner, D. (1992). *Managing at the speed of change: How resilient managers succeed and prosper where others fail*. New York: Random House.

Henderson, N., and M. Milstein (1996). *Resiliency in schools: Making it happen for students and educators*. Thousand Oaks, Calif.: Corwin Press.

Higgins, G. (1994). *Resilient adults: Overcoming a cruel past*. San Francisco: Jossey-Bass.

Kobasa, S. C. (1979). Stressful life events, personality, and health: An inquiry into hardiness. *Journal of Personality and Social Psychology* 37(1), 1–11.

Lieberman, A. (1992). School/university collaboration: A view from the inside. *Phi Delta Kappan* 74, 147–155.

Milstein, M., and D. A. Henry (1999). *Spreading resiliency: Making it happen for schools and community*. Thousand Oaks, Calif.: Corwin Press.

Operation Respect. *Don't laugh at me* (2000). 2 Penn Plaza, 23rd Floor, New York, N.Y. (Video)

Patterson, J. L. (1997). *Coming clean about organizational change*. Arlington, Va: American Association of School Administrators.

Patterson, J. L. (2000). *The anguish of leadership*. Arlington, VA: American Association of School Administrators.

Rosenholtz, S. J. (1991). *Teacher's workplace: The social organization of schools*. New York: Teachers College Press.

Rutter, M. (1984). Resilient children. *Psychology Today* (March), 57–65.

Rutter, M., B. Maughan, P. Mortimore, J. Ouston, and A. Smith (1979). *Fifteen thousand hours*. Cambridge: Harvard University Press.

Wasley, P. A. (1991). Teachers who lead: The rhetoric of reform and the realities of practice. New York: Teachers College Press.

Werner, E., and R. Smith (1992). *Overcoming the odds: High risk children from birth to adulthood*. Ithaca, N.Y.: Cornell University Press.

Whetten, D., and K. Cameron (1993). *Developing management skills: Communicating supportively*. New York: HarperCollins College Division.

Wolin, S., and S. Wolin (1993). *The resilient self: How survivors of troubled families rise above adversity*. New York: Villard.